Coaching
PLAIN & SIMPLE

A Norton Professional Book

Coaching
PLAIN & SIMPLE

SOLUTION-FOCUSED BRIEF COACHING ESSENTIALS

Peter Szabó and Daniel Meier

Translation by Kirsten Dierolf

W. W. Norton & Company
NEW YORK · LONDON

Note to Readers: Models and/or techniques described in this volume are illustrative or are included for general informational purposes only; neither the publisher nor the author(s) can guarantee the efficacy or appropriateness of any particular recommendation in every circumstance.

Copyright © 2008 by Solutionsurfers GmbH / Weiterbildungsforum
Translation copyright © 2009 by Peter Szabó, Daniel Meier, and Kirsten Dierolf

Originally published in German as
COACHING—ERFRISCHEND EINFACH:
Einführung ins lösungsorientierte Kurzzeitcoaching

For information about permission to reproduce selections
from this book, write to Permissions, W. W. Norton & Company, Inc.,
500 Fifth Avenue, New York, NY 10110

For information about special discounts for bulk
purchases, please contact W. W. Norton Special Sales at
specialsales@wwnorton.com or 800-233-4830

Book design by Carole Desnoes
Production manager: Devon Zahn

Library of Congress Cataloging-in-Publication Data

Szabo, Peter, 1957, Apr. 20–
[Coaching, erfrischend einfach. English]
Coaching plain & simple : solution-focused brief coaching essentials /
Peter Szabo and Daniel Meier ; translated by Kirsten Dierolf.
    p. cm. — (A Norton professional book)
Includes bibliographical references.
ISBN 978-0-393-70593-5 (pbk.)
1. Executive coaching. 2. Management. I. Meier, Daniel. II. Title.
III. Title: Coaching plain and simple.
HD30.4.S93 2009
658.3'124—dc22

                                2009001964

ISBN: 978-0-393-70593-5

W. W. Norton & Company, Inc
500 Fifth Avenue, New York, N.Y. 10110
www.wwnorton.com

W. W. Norton & Company Ltd.
15 Carlisle Street, London W1D 3BS

8 9 0

Contents

Coaching
PLAIN & SIMPLE

Introduction

Successful coaching does not necessarily need to continue for a long period of time. Maybe you have been asking yourself:

- Why is it that sometimes clients make dramatic progress in very little time?
- What is it that makes some of my coaching conversations so much more effective than others?

This is a book about the essential success factors of being brief and effective as a coach. You will find what we propose is surprisingly simple, especially compared to what other coaching approaches deem necessary. You can expect benefits such as being even more relaxed and minimalistic in your coaching, while getting increasing feedback about useful changes from your clients. You will gain new techniques as a coach and maybe leave behind some old ones. You will probably challenge your existing beliefs about how to be useful as a coach and open up a wider range of professional choices for yourself.

The solution-focused approach was developed in the early 1980s by a research group in Milwaukee including Insoo Kim Berg and Steve de Shazer. The group was driven to find something effective and efficient to help clients start successfully doing whatever they strive for. They began to experiment with "what might work" instead of finding "what caused the problem." By concentrating on building solutions, they were able to reduce the average consultation time by 70%—retaining the same success rate as more usual forms of therapy. They were not following a theoretical model. Instead, they researched their own conversations with a clear focus: Which questions and interventions led to useful results in the lives of clients? The simple conversational elements they came up with after many years of refining and further reduction represent a dramatic paradigm change in how to support sustainable progress.

In 1997 Peter Szabó started to transfer these solution-focused findings to the world of coaching. He founded a coaching school in Switzerland with the goal of adapting the tools and procedures from the therapeutic context and making them accessible for coaches and consultants in business and organizations. The result is called solution-focused coaching or brief coaching.

Daniel Meier later developed a solution-focused model for coaching teams. He also adapted brief coaching techniques for a management context.

Solutionsurfers, based in Lucerne, and founded by Peter and Daniel, has since become the number one coach training institute in Switzerland, and we now deliver brief coaching training courses all over the globe. After more than 10 years of experience in teaching and practicing coaching, we thought it was time to write this plain and simple book on solution-focused brief coaching. You will find a short introduction, all the necessary tools, and the central assumptions behind this refreshingly new and different coaching approach.

Enjoy!

Peter Szabó and Daniel Meier
Solutionsurfers, Lucerne, September 2008

What Is Coaching?

We are often asked, "So what exactly is coaching? What do you do as a coach all day?" In fact, we can sometimes see a slight ironic smile on the face of the person who is asking. The word *coaching* is indeed widely used—from management support services to the lady in our fitness club who introduces herself as a wellness coach. For clarity, we will explain what we mean by coaching in this book.

Creating a Framework for Solutions

In a neighboring Swiss town, you can still find a real frame maker. When you stand in front of his shop, through the shop window you can see undecorated frames, partially or fully gilded frames, frames with artistic carvings, colored, black, metal, and wooden frames: a large selection. Innumerable frames seem to be waiting, each for its own picture. Often we only recognize the colors and perspectives, the lighting and the message of a work of art when it is placed in an appropriate frame. Rembrandt was quoted as saying that during his whole career it was more difficult for him to find an appropriate frame than to paint the picture. Framing a picture in such a way that it can unfold its full expressivity is an art that few people have mastered.

The arts and crafts of frame making and coaching have a lot in common for us. As coaches we create a frame (of thought) for the client in which his or her goals, solutions, and first steps can shine. The frame constructed by the coach consists of goal-oriented questions, reinforcing feedback, present listening, and useful summary. The client can take space and time to sort out his or her thoughts, set concrete goals, become aware of resources, and plan next steps. It is the task of the coach to ensure that each client receives the appropriate frame. But just like the frame maker, the coach would never start actively creating the picture.

Coaching in Action:
A Butterfly Does Not Have to Fight—Emergency Coaching in the Evening

One evening, I found Beatrice M.'s* message on my cell phone voice mail. I had met Beatrice a few months before in one of my team workshops. Beatrice worked as head of a service department in a large bank. Her voice sounded desperate: Could I please call back this evening—no matter the time. She was waiting for my call. She needed an emergency coaching session to save her job.

I called her around 9 p.m. after my workshop. She said that she did not know what to do. That afternoon she had received an e-mail from the secretary of her new boss containing a PowerPoint presentation with the new structure of the division. She could not find herself and her department in this structure. It had simply disappeared. At first, Beatrice had hidden in her office and then had tried twice to phone her boss but to no avail. I noticed that she was close to tears when she told me how mean and insulting she found all this and how she really had trouble with this kind of corporate culture. She told me about her previous boss, who valued her work and gave her a lot of appreciation and room to maneuver. I asked Beatrice how I could support her now, in this moment. Beatrice hoped to plan her next steps together with me.

---

*All coaching examples are from our practice. All names and organizations were changed for confidentiality reasons.

How should she deal with the situation? At the moment, so she thought, she really did not know what to do.

> Beatrice: And I really need to know tomorrow, better tonight, what I am going to do. I have to be quick—otherwise I am out of the picture! I won't let them chase me off like this.
>
> Coach: Listening to you, I ask myself whether there have been situations in your life that were as difficult as this one that you were able to manage successfully.

Beatrice remembered two situations in which she had fought for her department and her project "like a lioness"—with great success. But she said again and again that she had fought with passion at that time—and that today there was only anger. Today, she was too tired to generate energy and act out of this anger.

I said, "Looking at the situation and what you have discovered and said just now, what would you like instead of this anger?"

There was a moment of silence on the other end of the telephone line.

> Beatrice: I want to be able to do my work calmly and with ease. I want to receive some appreciation for it and pass on appreciation. Calm and with ease—working like a butterfly.
>
> Coach: It's not yet clear to me—what is your goal exactly? What does the flower look like that the butterfly would like to land on? [Again, silence.]
>
> Beatrice: A butterfly doesn't have to fight to do its work! What has become clear for me now is that I no longer want to fight. I am tired and don't want to have to prove constantly that I am competent. Tomorrow, when I am talking to my boss, I will try to find good positions for my eight team members in the new organization . . . but I don't really want to work there

3

any longer. The best would really be if I could give myself the luxury of taking 2 or 3 months off to find out what kind of new job would really fit me.

After Beatrice had become aware of her new goal, her next steps were also clear to her. During the coaching and with the frame that the coaching created, she was able to order her thoughts, which had been muddled at the beginning. She could renew her focus on what she really wanted and delineate clear goals from that. Beatrice used the time to make important decisions for herself.

We used the last minutes of the coaching conversation to look at her decision to resign from different angles and at what was giving her the confidence to dare to take this step. Desperation made way for cautious hope and confidence in the future.

Three weeks after our conversation, Beatrice wrote a short e-mail telling me that she had been able to find good positions for seven of her eight team members and that the eighth person was currently in the process of internal application. Her boss had actually even wanted to keep Beatrice on for a strategic project and give her the lead on it, but Beatrice stood by her resignation. She wrote, "I am looking forward to my time as a butterfly!"

Making a Difference in Awareness, Choice, and Trust

The example of Beatrice helps us further elaborate the term *coaching*. Coaching should primarily be defined by its effects. A coaching client only pays because the conversation creates useful effects for him or her. We like to go along with Tim Gallway,[*] who structured the effects of coaching into three areas, as shown in the figure.

---

[*] W. Timothy Gallway was one of the earliest coaches in the United States to discover the power of focusing awareness and utilizing it consistently, especially in the sports world (cf. *The Inner Game of Tennis*). (Gallway, *The Inner Game of Work*, Random House, 2000, p. 48)

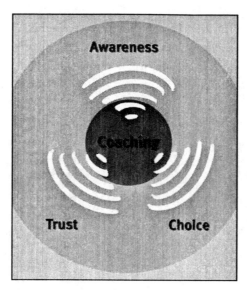

Effects of Coaching

Raising Awareness

Awareness is a bit like the light of a flashlight. Whatever we direct the beam toward becomes visible in the dark. Oftentimes coaching clients come to us with a flashlight that directs its beam toward a problem—and all the rest is in darkness. That is what it was like for Beatrice. In her desperation, she saw only the impossible behavior of her boss, who had simply eradicated her and her department without even talking to her or preparing her for it. Beatrice could only feel her disappointment and anger about it.

The questions of her coach enabled her to widen the beam of her flashlight. For example, she discovered how she had been able to do something useful in a similar situation in the past. By shedding light on her goals, she became clear on how to utilize the situation for herself.

By widening the beam of the flashlight and shedding light on new and useful areas for the client, facets and details become visible that had previously been in the dark. The focus of awareness of the client also widens. The client can perceive other parts of his or her reality and redescribe it and thus generate more options. The client leaves the conversation with a different awareness.

Increasing Choice

At the beginning, Beatrice was so caught up in her problem that she did not see any possibility of doing something useful. Concrete small steps were hardly imaginable for her.

Sometimes a client comes to a coach with the question of whether he or she should do A or B—and he or she does not see any alternatives to A or B, although neither A nor B are really satisfactory solutions.

In a coaching conversation, clients can gain new options and discover that they can develop their own ideas. Often this leads clients to discover that they are able to create and influence their own future and are not simply victims of circumstance. They become aware of their expanded choices.

Strengthening Confidence

One very central effect of coaching consists of clients' increased self-confidence and confidence in their own abilities to master a difficult situation. Confidence is a prerequisite for taking small steps for change—if you trust in yourself, you will be able to try something new and different. The coaching conversation creates a framework in which the client becomes aware of his or her competencies and resources and is able to access them. Confidence is the key for utilizing your own resources. In the example, Beatrice became aware of the competencies that she had previously used to master situations that were as difficult as the one at hand. She rediscovered her potential in the conversation with the coach. Rediscovering your own abilities stengthens your confidence and conviction, which enables you to take concrete steps in the direction of your goals.

Supporting Customized Change

In our understanding, the coach supports the client in his or her creation of solutions. This process of creating solutions remains the responsibility of the client. This is why coaching leads to fitting results in implementation. Coaching always aims at helping someone to help themselves. In this process, successful coaches make themselves more and more superfluous. Success happens when the client gets closer to his or her goals and the coach is no longer necessary.

The best solutions are not custom made—
they are customer-made.
—Mike Goran

We like to define coaching like this: "Bringing an important person from where he or she is to where he or she wants to go." We have come to cherish this definition because it elegantly describes an element of coaching that we deem a central characteristic of coaching conversations.

The definition states: "where he or she wants to go." It is not the coach who determines where the journey will lead but the client. Therefore, one of the most important tasks of the coach is to take enough time to enable clients to clarify their goals and the effects of reaching those goals. Clients explore their goals, their solutions, and their paths toward those goals, which ensures that the coaching develops individual, customized solutions that can be implemented. The most helpful turning point for Beatrice happened when she was able to formulate what she really wanted: "To work calmly and with ease." From that moment on, the next steps were clearly visible and easy to define.

Thus coaching might have to do with the original meaning of the word *coach*: a coachman or cab driver who supports customers in getting from where they are to their desired destination.

At the end of each chapter, we would like to encourage you to verify what we have written in your own practice and to have your own experiences with the brief coaching ideas. This is why we have created a little experiment in each chapter for you to try out.

In our understanding, coaching is a very individual art. These experiments might help you manifest your own individual coaching style and support your own learning.

EXPERIMENT

Find out about the effects of your coaching. Toss a coin and when it comes up heads, ask your client at the end of the session to allow you to do a bit of research:

- How are things different for you (the client) after the conversation in comparison to before the conversation?
- What has been particularly helpful during this session?

Keep a list of answers and observe how it might influence your coaching.

2

Useful Assumptions
for Being Brief

If solution-focused brief coaching practices what it preaches, the coaching process should be completed in a rather short time. But what is it that helps to keep a coaching relationship brief? What can we coaches do to enable the client to reach sustainable solutions quickly?

One the one hand, we make certain useful assumptions that help us in this endeavor, as we will explain in the following paragraphs. On the other hand, we use a tried and tested set of coaching tools and a conversation structure that support the coach in keeping the relationship brief. We describe these instruments in the following chapters.

Our assumptions influence our actions—and this is also valid for brief coaching. Next we present four helpful assumptions central to brief coaching.

Assumption 1: Solution Building Is a Fast Track to Problem Solving

At first glance, the distinction between solution building and problem solving does not seem very big—however, in brief coaching practice, this difference is crucial.

Clients usually approach a coach when they are confronted with a problem that they cannot solve on their own, where they are stuck. It is common sense to assume that we have to analyze the problem carefully to be able to find a suitable solution. So if, for example, a head of a department is complaining about stress in the office and tells the coach about sleepless nights and often feeling tired and having no energy, the coach would ask, "Why?" The attempt to understand where these problems originate is founded in the assumption that by explaining the problem a solution can be found.

Our experience in brief coaching shows that we can help clients reach sustainable results much more easily if we follow a different procedure. We support clients in building as much as possible of their desired solution using target-oriented questions and interventions. Most of the time in the coaching session is used to find out more about clients' goals, expected positive effects, and previous successes—the analysis of the problem is completely neglected.

In brief coaching, we assume that the solution has nothing to do with the problem. To put it provocatively: The solution does not care why the problem occurred.

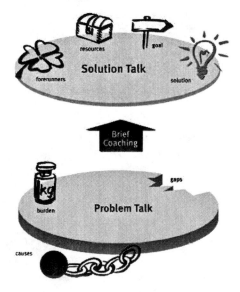

In brief coaching we spend a lot of time with solution talk.

It is your own choice what kind of awareness you want to foster. You can use questions to create awareness of the problem in your client—in this case you will most probably ask questions starting with "why." You will discover new facets of the problem together with your client and you will discover that the situation is really difficult. Or you can aim at strengthening the awareness of solutions. Then you will ask about the goal, existing resources, and about first small successes.

We often discover that questions that strengthen the awareness of solutions in a way clear the air and rekindle energy in the client. This first assumption—the coach helps to create awareness of solutions in the client—may seem a bit abstract. We would therefore like to give you an example that our British colleague Harry Norman told us.

Coaching in Action:
Anxiety Attacks in the Office

An administrative assistant, Jane, approached Harry in the context of a larger coaching contract and asked him for a coaching conversation. She told him that she was having anxiety attacks in the office and described hot flashes and being short of breath.

Following a more classic approach, the coach might ask for the reason why and would try to find out where these attacks came from, assuming that by finding an explanation a possible solution can be found. The coach would start with a working hypothesis that there is a connection between the cause of the problem and the solution. In the coaching literature you can find questions for this purpose, for example:

- How exactly does the problem manifest itself in your daily life?
- Where do you think it comes from?
- Imagine you are in the situation in which the problem occurs. Describe your perceptions. What do you see, feel, and so on?
- Do you think these attacks could be part of an old pattern that you have to be perfect?

This analysis usually leads to a plan with various actions and tasks. In the above example of anxiety attacks, the coach would try to find out what triggered the attack. He would possibly conclude that Jane is lacking some knowledge or competencies to fulfill her demanding tasks. In this case he would recommend that she attend a few training sessions to acquire such knowledge or skills. Or the coach would find out that Jane's boss is a very unpleasant and moody person. If this is the reason, Jane should try to resolve her issues with her boss first. Or it would become clear that fear is at the root of the problem. Then coach and client could start working on the fear. Maybe the coach would also say, "Oh, I think this is a case for long-term therapy. I don't think there is anything I can do as a coach!"

Harry Norman responded to Jane's request. In their coaching conversation, he asked two crucial questions:

- If your problem was solved, what exactly would be different?
- What are some times in which these attacks do not happen?

On the basis of these questions, Jane was able to imagine or invent a future situation in which she would really like her work. She got the opportunity, the time, and the interested attention of the coach to describe the optimal situation in which her goal would be reached. Answering the second question, she remarked, to her own and also to Harry's surprise, that the optimal situation was already occurring—and that this always happened on Tuesdays. On Tuesdays, Jane went to lunch with a colleague that she really liked. This lunch obviously somehow— we don't really know exactly how—helped Jane to achieve her optimal state. After the conversation, Jane organized more lunches with nice colleagues, which actually had the desired effect.

Albert Einstein once said something that applies to this story really well: "No problem can be solved from the same level of consciousness as the one that created it."

One of the central differences of brief coaching from other coaching models is that we mainly work on creating an awareness of the solution. Our questions lead the client to switch from exploring the level of the problem to exploring the level of solutions. Harry Norman demonstrated this switch with only one question—the question about the desired future solution state.

Additionally, we hardly have to know anything about the initial problem situation. We can create new realities with simple goal-oriented questions; realities that are not only more bearable but that also open up completely new options and choices for the client.

Assumption 2: Clients Already Have Experience With the Solution

Jane's example shows that it was very useful to find out what had already worked—and this is another assumption of brief coaching: No problem exists all the time and with the same intensity. There are times in which the problem does not occur, or happens only in a mild form. As coaches we trust in the fact that clients already have some experience with the solution, that they have already experienced shorter or longer phases in which the difficulty was less pronounced or did not happen at all.

No problem exists all the time—
or all the time with the same intensity.
What happens the rest of the time?
How can we use these experiences
to develop a solution?

As coaches, we can become interested in finding out how clients manage to create these problem-free times. What is their contribution? Which resources help enable them to experience these little exceptions? The discoveries can be important signposts for developing a solution. Steve de Shazer said, "If it works, do more of it!" This should remind us coaches to take our clients on a careful resource walk into the past and look for small and large harbingers of the desired solution.

In the example, it was helpful for Jane to remind herself of the regular lunch date with her colleague. Admittedly, this was a surprisingly simple discovery. But why should we not use it to support Jane in creating a better work life for herself? Why not find out whether it was possible to control her anxiety attacks by having more lunch dates? At the third session, Jane reported that the attacks had almost completely vanished within a month after the follow-up coaching. Jane herself decided that this was good enough and that she did not need any further coaching.

Assumption 3: When in Doubt, Trust the Client

Coaching is necessarily about finding customized solutions, solutions that fit the customer completely—not just any solutions. Our coaching clients are knowledgeable about their own (subjective) worlds, which are absolutely unique. The client is expert in his or her worlds. The experiences of the coach and his or her good ideas and pieces of advice always stay his or her own. They will never completely fit the world of the client. This is why we do not give advice or hints in brief coaching but enable clients to work on their own individual solutions and to continue fine-tuning until they really fit.

"Don't fix it, if it's not broken!" In brief coaching, the customer determines what needs to be repaired, not the coach. Many coaches who work with other models try to understand what might be behind the problem: lack of self-confidence, deep underlying fear, or difficulties in communication. Then they start working on these topics rather than on the initial request of the client. In our practice, we do not consider it useful to construct such assumptions about the client.

Instead, we honor the customer as an expert without having to invent any background or explanation for his or her behavior. We work on what customers deem important, look at their behavior and actions, and think about how they would like to act in the future. Finding a label for these actions or finding out where the problem comes from is not relevant for being brief and effective. We consciously stay on the surface and work only and exactly with what the customer wants to work on. This is why we like the term *customer*—it is about customized solutions that fit the customs of our customers.

If we see clients as experts on their own lives, we as coaches need to trust the resources and competencies of our clients. This trust is probably the most central premise of solution-focused work. The coach assumes that the customer possesses all the necessary competencies to come to a solution. Even more to the point: The coach even assumes that the client has already experienced the solution but simply forgot to notice. Coaching creates a frame in which clients can focus their attention on the areas of their experience. If we are successful in directing the attention of the client to these areas, competencies can most often be activated and used intentionally even if they had not been perceived by the client for a long time.

We are grateful to Sir John Whitmore, who introduced the following metaphor about coaching.*

The oak seed has stored in itself all the necessary information
to grow into a big strong tree.

* A book recommendation: Sir John Whitmore developed the widespread GROW-Coaching model. John Whitmore, *Coaching for Performance*, Nicholas Brealey, 2002.

Peter's story of becoming a coach reflects both ways of looking at customers:

For a long time, I worked as the head of training and development in a large insurance company. I remember very well how I strolled through the hallways and offices looking for empty water glasses among the employees. From the viewpoint of the training and development manager, it was necessary to spot the employees' deficits in skills and competencies in order to determine which types of training to design and offer. Deficits in communication, time management, and so on, that I noticed, seemed to me like empty water glasses and the training that our department customized for this deficit was the liquid necessary to fill what was obviously missing.

There could not be a larger contrast with the viewpoint of a coach: A coach sees the oak seed and knows that all the potential, all necessary information to let it grow into a large and powerful oak tree are already contained in the seed. For me, the former training and development manager looking to fill water glasses, becoming a coach meant a large change in perspective. Now it was about examining the oak seed in order to find out if there might be even the smallest crack. And then the only things I needed were some patience and fine-tuning in order to notice the first small signs (not even green, white at first) of what was growing in the direction of the light. The image of the oak seed signifies that there is nothing that needs to be added. Everything is already there, and the only thing that I can do as a coach is hold a time and space for it to grow.

It is one of the most fascinating and rewarding experiences as a coach to be a witness when customers rediscover their resources, activate them, and find solutions to their questions in full self-confidence.

Assumption 4: Not Knowing Is Useful

Being a brief coach is very demanding: holding back one's own ideas, not developing hypotheses about causes and possible deficits, actually staying out of the content part of the conversation and at the same time trusting the client, only steering the process—that isn't easy.

In this context, we often say that the coach can practice the art of not knowing. In contrast to today's tendency to collect extensive and well-founded knowledge, not knowing is an important coaching competency. We meet our clients without previous assumptions or prejudices, without value judgments, and this gives us something akin to the freedom of a court jester, which enables us to ask unconventional questions. We leave the responsibility for the content to the expert—the customer. The opposite of not knowing is certainty. We generally tend to like to gain certainty, to find convincing arguments, to analyze thoroughly to find the "truth." Don't we all want to corroborate our statements with good thinking and well-researched data? But what seems obvious for us is only our construction, our view on the world. Taking on our viewpoint is no real solution for our clients. The art of not knowing helps the coach concentrate on his job, which is creating a useful coaching process, posing helpful questions, listening appreciatively, giving resource-oriented feedback, and—as one of our coaching colleagues is known to say—not getting in the way of miracles.

Some people find supporting coaching customers with a not-knowing stance challenging and energy-consuming. We have discovered that if you have mastered the art, coaching becomes what the Swiss call "a Schoggi job"—a chocolate job. Coaches can lean back, pose useful, goal-oriented questions, and enjoy the answers of the client as if they were just enjoying a piece of chocolate. This is truly a

There is no true understanding of what clients really want to tell us. There are only more or less useful misunderstandings.
—Steve de Shazer

chocolate job. It is the client who works in the coaching conversation and who designs fitting solutions. The coach remains laid-back and enjoys the freedom of the court jester because he or she does not have to know about or even understand the content. The coach can completely trust the expert knowledge of the customer.

EXPERIMENT

To keep coaching brief, it can be useful to be aware of your assumptions. We invite you to reflect on the following regarding your current customers:

- On a scale of 1 to 10: How confident are you that your clients have everything they need to build their own solutions?
- Suppose you fully believed your client is the expert for his or her own solutions. How would you coach differently? How would your client notice?

Overview: Elements of a Solution-Focused Conversation

There are five central elements of a brief coaching conversation, which you will encounter throughout this book. In a first coaching session, these elements might provide you with an easy-to-follow structure, like phases of a typical conversation, where the next element logically builds on the first one. Nevertheless we like to look at them as separate pieces that can be freely chosen or combined, depending on what seems most useful for the client.

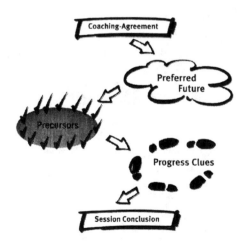

Elements of a brief coaching conversation.

Element 1: Coaching Agreement

The coaching agreement phase serves to clarify what would be a useful result for the client at the end of the first conversation. There is an agreement about the goal and the content of the conversation.

Central Question

"What needs to happen here today, so that you can say that it was worth your time?"

Element 2: Preferred Future

In this phase, we invite clients to see beyond eventual obstacles and explore the consequences of having reached the goal. Clients become clear on which differences will really make a difference in their preferred future.

Central Questions

"Suppose there is a miracle overnight that solves the problems or challenges you brought into this session. How will you start to discover the next morning that the miracle must have happened?"

Element 3: Precursors of the Solution

Here we presuppose that valuable pieces of the preferred future already exist in the client's life at present or in the recent past. It is important to identify the contribution of the client that made these precursors of the solution possible and to find out which personal skills and resources helped him or her to do it.

Central Questions

"Which situations in the recent past contained at least a small piece of your preferred future already happening? How did you do that?"

Element 4: Clues for Upcoming Progress

The presupposition embedded in this element is that the client's progress is inevitable. So we take time for clients to find out how they will recognize clear signs of their progress and also establish first concrete steps, if appropriate.

Central Questions

"Where are you now on a scale of 1 to 10? Ten means that you have reached your goal completely and 1 means the opposite. How will you notice that you are just one step higher on the scale? And how else?"

Element 5: Session Conclusion

Apart from the obvious, like clarifying how to proceed in the future, two elements are significant for the last phase of the conversation:

- Appreciation from the coach for what has already been achieved and acknowledgment of the client's resources,
- An experiment suggested by the coach aimed at supporting the client in the implementation of the first steps.

We would like to finish this overview with two remarks from our practice.

First, the above five elements of a brief coaching conversation are our inventions as a support for our learning and understanding. Of course every coaching conversation is unique, not repeatable, and different from any conversation before or after it. Most often we have to adapt our questions to this uniqueness. Often we cannot clearly separate the individual elements from one another. Sometimes they flow naturally into one another or a different sequence turns out to be more appropriate.

Second, these five elements are what we mean by plain and simple coaching. In our daily practice, even with complex and urgent client issues, so far there has been no need to add or change much. On the contrary: exactly this simplicity of sticking to five simple tools seems to support both the briefness of the process and the sustainability of the results. In the following chapters, you will find many real-life examples of how it works.

4

Contacting
Before You Start

Most often there is a first contact between client and coach before the first coaching conversation happens. A customer calls you, or someone approaches you during a workshop or at a conference. What are good ways of interacting before you even start the first coaching conversation?

Coaching in Action:
Journalist Steve B., Part 1

I was giving a workshop on the topic of solution-focused coaching at a conference when I was approached by a man in his 40s who was asking for a quick word. Steve B. told me that he was a journalist and that he was currently in a desperate situation in his job. He was being sued for an article he had written. His reputation and his career as a journalist were in danger. He was unsure that the management of the newspaper he was writing for was actually supporting him, nor did he know whether he could trust the lawyer that management had selected to represent him.

Steve asked me to keep our conversation absolutely confidential. He wanted to be coached by me because he was desperate and at the end of his rope. He was afraid that the lawsuit could ruin his professional and private future. The fact that he did not know how to deal with the people who were involved made him feel very insecure.

This was obviously an urgent situation and we were both expecting a longer term coaching relationship.

We agreed on the first telephone coaching session and set a date and time for the next evening at 8 p.m. so that we would have enough undisturbed time for the conversation. I informed Steve about my fees and explained that I charge for the first conversation, but that he would not have to pay should the conversation turn out to be of no use to him.

The first contact in brief coaching may look like this. In the following, you will find some useful hints for the first contact when working with a brief coaching model.

FOR YOUR TOOLKIT

Hints for clarifying the contract:

- **Goal:** Clarify the goal of the client during the first contact. Inquire about expected consequences of reaching the goal and especially discuss how the client will notice that the coaching has come to a successful end.
- **Number of coaching conversations:** Explain that you are working with a brief coaching model and that the goal can sometimes be reached in a very short time. Respect the perception of your client who might have suffered for a long time already and is therefore expecting that it will take a long time to solve the problem. Remember that you cannot possibly predict at this point when things will become "good enough" for the client with no further need for coaching. It doesn't make a lot of sense to determine a fixed number of appointments at the beginning. Whether or not the next session is necessary can be decided at the end of each session on the basis of the progress achieved.

- **Fee for the first conversation:** Explain that in brief coaching you charge for the first session since you start the coaching process right away. Our customers often tell us about coaches who do not charge for the first session. This makes sense if you have a long-term coaching relationship where you bill monthly. The first session in these kinds of processes mainly serves the purpose of information exchange. This does not seem practical for brief coaching, which has an average of two or three sessions.

EXPERIMENT

How does the expectation of the coach influence what happens during the coaching? If you find this question interesting, we have an experiment for you to try out with your next new client.

After you have a contract, make a prediction about the number of necessary sessions with this particular client. Take note of the number you deem necessary and think of a little reward for yourself if your prediction turns out to be correct.

Repeat the experiment if you find it useful.

5

Reaching a
Coaching Agreement

Part of what you want to accomplish during a first session is obviously to find out what the client wants to accomplish: "What needs to happen here today, so that at the end of our conversation you can say it was worth your time?"

Starting With the End in Mind

There are many possible ways to start a first session. In brief coaching, we make a deliberate choice by starting with the end in mind. This is different from starting with the present or past, which would involve questions like, "How would you describe your current situation? Who is involved? What is the problem? Where does it come from? Why is it so?" A colleague of ours calls such questions "reporter questions." They simply provide the coach with information about the issue and its implications that the client already knows. Instead of such reporter questions, we prefer to ask coaching questions that are more useful to provide clients with solution-focused new insights.

Beginning with the end in mind can support customers in strongly connecting with what they want to accomplish right from the start:

- Suppose our coaching has ended successfully and you will somehow have managed to solve whatever brought you to me. How will that make a difference for you?

Coach and client can explore how the daily actions of the client will change. Also they should carefully explore the concrete signs that will tell the customer that the coaching relationship can be terminated:

- How will you know for sure that things have become sufficiently better so that you need no further coaching?

Problem talk creates problems.
Solution talk creates solutions.
—Steve de Shazer

Coaching in Action:
Journalist Steve B., Part 2

I said, "What needs to happen here this evening so that it was worth taking your time for the conversation?"

Of course, Steve first took several minutes to inform me about the newest developments in his case, which actually were quite alarming. His wife, who was normally very patient and understanding, was starting to suffer and was complaining about the fact that Steve's mind seemed to be elsewhere all the time. Steve was also very concerned about possibly not being able to make enough money to support his family. Apart from the tensions in his private life, there was also the issue with the newspaper and the lawsuit, which wasn't really moving forward.

After I repeated my original question about what needed to happen, Steve answered that he would need to do much less of the less important things, that he would need ideas about how to tackle the lawsuit, and that he wanted to think realistically about his professional future and somehow find the peace and energy to take things into his own hands.

At first, I simply repeated this hasty list. I said, "So suppose for a moment you somehow have tackled all this. You have managed to sort out the issues somehow, you have taken things into your own hands, and you have found the necessary peace and energy. How would you notice that things are good enough so that we can end our coaching relationship?"

A long pause ensued. Then Steve said that his wife and kids being more relaxed would probably be a clear sign of his being back on track. This would probably be due to Steve having his inner balance back: "It is like my confidence would tell me that I did everything I could. I could just let go of those things that I simply cannot change anyway."

While he was following these thoughts, something astonishing happened. Our coaching conversation had only lasted 10 minutes. But something in the way in which he was describing the first signs that would tell him he could stop being alarmed and the sound of his voice made me wonder. It seemed as if some significant change had happened. I wanted to check this, so I asked a little bit reluctantly, "When I'm listening to how you just said that, I wonder: Could it be that things are good enough for you already?" He said that he had just asked himself the same question. He almost could not believe how clear everything suddenly had become for him. He knew the things he would do next and he was also clear about his priorities for the next 72 hours. He said something like a 180-degree change had happened. "To be honest," he said, "I am very surprised." Now I have enough confidence that I can deal with the issues myself and in my way. Thank you very much for the coaching!"

With a total duration of about 15 minutes, this was definitely the shortest coaching relationship that I ever had in a professional context. When I met Steve accidentally a year later, we talked for a few minutes. I didn't explicitly ask about the state of the lawsuit. Steve was telling me enthusiastically about his current journalistic projects. I was content to assume that obviously the coaching might have somehow been helpful. Steve apparently must have taken things into his own hands after the conversation and had reached a sustainable solution.

Of course, this is a rather extraordinary example of how short brief coaching can actually be if you start by talking about what the end should look like. But it is not so rare that coaching ends the moment a client is clear on what he or she really wants. Agreeing early on about observable clues for ending the coaching is a very good way of keeping the coaching relationship short. The coaching agreement is not just about gathering information; it can also be a powerful intervention to invite the client out of being stuck. As Steve B. began to have the wanted outcome in mind, he got back into resourceful solution consciousness.

Brief coaching typically has the purpose of supporting clients to start moving in a useful direction. The coach assumes that once the first step is made, one step will lead to another. We presuppose that clients are competent and experienced enough to find their own way once they have started moving in the desired direction. The main focus in brief coaching is not accompanying the client the whole way from A to B. It is mainly about helping him or her to make a good start toward a solution.

FOR YOUR TOOLKIT

Questions for starting with the end in mind:

- How will you notice that things are good enough and that it is time to end the coaching relationship?
- What would you like to achieve by the end of this session?
- How will other people notice that things are good enough now?
- What is the first small sign that tells you that you can manage to proceed on your own from here on?

Question for clients who know what they do not want:

- What would you rather do instead?

A clear agreement helps you and your client enter into an effective, mutually accepted working relationship.

It Takes Two to Tango

In our closing remarks for this chapter, we would like to stress that the chapter title contains the word *agreement*, which usually involves at least two parties. This means that you as a coach also need to agree to something. Finding out what the client wants is only one part of the agreement. In this negotiation, you can also freely decide whether or not you want to deliver your services depending on the client, the issue at hand, and your personal level of comfort with the situation. Coaches have the right to decline. There might be ethical, professional, or personal reasons for doing so. Being professional also means that you are aware of the exit sign. At this point in the brief coaching, we communicate where we stand. It is basically either "Yes, I would like to work with you on this" or "I am not the best resource for your goal. Can I help you find someone who is a better fit?"

We would like to direct your thoughts toward your own future for a moment. This experiment is about your learning as a coach.

Imagine for a moment that we had written all of the following pages of this book especially for you and your learning desires. You find all the content on coaching that you have always been looking for. Reading this book therefore surpasses your wildest expectations.

- How would having read the book make a difference to you?
- What would you be doing differently in your coaching practice after reading the book?
- How would your clients notice that you have found what you had always been looking for?

6

Discovering a
Preferred Future

When they come to coaching, clients often do not have a clear view of where they would like to be at the end of the coaching relationship. A problem, obstacle, or challenge seems to be obstructing their vision.

Seeing Beyond the Obstacles

In brief coaching, examining the obstacle is not important. Instead, we use this element of the coaching conversation to jump over this obstacle into what will come beyond it—into what we call the preferred future (the time when the client will have reached his or her goal). In our conversations, it has proven useful to spend a lot of time talking about the preferred future. It enables the customer to create a very concrete picture of his or her goal and to discover the personal longings linked to reaching the goal. Usually the goal becomes more attractive and clients seem to connect more with their resources.

There are different ways of exploring the preferred future. We often use a so-called miracle question, especially if the issue seems hopeless in the beginning and it seems that it would take a miracle to fix it. Here is an example.

Coaching in Action:
Ms. K.: A Professional Challenge at 55

When Ms. K. called, she told me that her work situation had become almost unbearable after a reorganization in her company. She was now the assistant to two superiors rather than just one. Both were making her life miserable and neither gave her any appreciation for her work at all. She was also no longer allowed to work independently. To make things worse, her chances of finding a new position at age 55 were almost zero, given the difficult situation in the job market at the time. Since she was single, she depended on her own income.

The coaching consisted of two telephone conversations of about 45 minutes each. There were approximately 2 weeks between them. During the second conversation, Ms. K. reported that her work situation had improved so significantly that she was thinking about staying in the company. We had agreed on a third conversation. However, it lasted only 5 minutes, in which she explained that she had had an interview with another company that had given her so much self-confidence that she did not see a need for another coaching session, even if she did not end up being offered the new position.

During our first session there had been no expectation of such an astonishing development and no reason for optimism. At that time Ms. K. was hopelessly stuck in an unbearable job, and there seemed to be no light at the end of the tunnel. In the first coaching session, I asked her what her goal for that session would be and she said that she would either like to find out how to bear her current situation (which she thought was completely impossible) or that she would like to develop possibilities for finding a new position (which to her seemed unrealistic due to the situation in the job market).

When I asked Ms. K. what would be different if one or both of her goals were reached, she said that she really did not know—but that it would be a real miracle. "And it would take a huge miracle to get there," she added with a deep sigh.

Coach: Okay, then let me ask you a somewhat strange and extraordinary question which requires a little bit of imagination. Suppose our conversation is over. You hang up the phone, and you do whatever you have planned for the rest of the evening; maybe you eat something, and then

> *Our desires are the harbinger of the*
> *capabilities that rest within us.*
> *They are the forerunners of what*
> *we will be able to do . . . ; we feel a*
> *longing for what we already secretly possess.*
> *Thus passionately imagining a future in our dreams*
> *turns what is possible into reality.*
> *—Johann Wolfgang von Goethe*

you might do something else . . . and sometime this evening you get tired and you go to bed. In the middle of the night, while you're fast asleep, a miracle happens. And the miracle is that everything that you brought to this coaching session is solved somehow . . . just like that. When you wake up the next morning, you do not know that there has been a miracle because you were fast asleep and nobody tells you that a miracle happened. So when you wake up tomorrow morning, how will you start discovering that a miracle actually happened?

Ms. K.: Well, I think I would wake up and look forward to the working day. I would look into the mirror and see a competent, appreciated woman who does her job well—and I would be aware of all of my resources!

Coach: Oh, I see! What else would be different in the morning or the day after the miracle?

Ms. K. said that she would be able to keep a healthy distance even on the job and she would be looking after herself better. At this point I thoroughly explored how she would behave differently and what she would do after the miracle that she wasn't doing now.

Ms. K.: Since I would have more energy and enthusiasm, I would probably call an old friend of mine and go to dinner with her. I haven't done that in months. I decline all invitations because I am so exhausted.

Coach: After the miracle, if you go to dinner with a friend who knows you well, how will the friend notice that the miracle happened to you (without you telling her)?

We spent some time on a detailed description of her possible actions and the observable differences that these actions produce. Ms. K. generated lively descriptions within the context of her real life about how she would act more self-confidently toward her superiors.

> Coach: How would you know that your superiors also noticed that you are more self-confident without you telling them openly? Let's take Dr. F. first. How would you know that he noticed?
>
> Ms. K.: I think Dr. F. would be a little bit more polite. Maybe he would say "hello" or "please." Possibly he would also praise me about something—this would be a huge miracle—and I would surely know that he has noticed that he is dealing with a competent woman who deserves respect.
>
> Coach: Suppose he said something nice about your work. How would you react?
>
> Ms. K.: I would probably smile and say that I am happy about it. And to myself I would say "bingo" and would reward myself by going to the sauna in the evening.

The Miracle Question in Slow Motion

Gift Wrapping the Question

Sometimes the miracle question seems to us like a valuable present to our customers. In order to prepare them for the wonderful gift, we package it carefully.

> Let me ask you a somewhat strange and extraordinary question which requires a little bit of imagination . . .

Ms. K. had already spent a lot of time thinking about her problem. Although she mentions a miracle, she probably never dared to really think about it. She has good reasons to think that dealing with her problem first is more urgent than thinking about a miracle. Therefore, announcing that the next question will be a little bit strange and extraordinary can be a helpful preparation.

Suppose . . .

This is the magic word that starts the careful construction of a bridge. In the context of this type of coaching, this word bridges two completely different perspectives that previously had no connection to one another. On one side of the bridge, our client is confronted with strong obstacles in her work life, and nobody can know whether she will be able to surpass them. In order to build the bridge in that moment, we do nothing but simply suppose that her problems have been solved—just like that.

There are two important elements in the preferred future: First, we offer our clients the possibility of finding out what their world would look like if their problems were solved, just  *like that—as if the miracle had happened. In the second part of the preferred future, it is helpful to carefully explore the consequences of the miracle for daily actions. What consequences does the solution state have for the behavior of the customer and also for his or her environment?*

You go home, and you do whatever you have planned for the rest of the evening.

Evidently we need to take some time cross the bridge. We start on this side of the bridge, embedded in the safe reality of the daily life of our client. Of course, Ms. K. will go home after the coaching conversation, and she will do something in the evening, maybe iron or watch television.

In the middle of the night while you're fast asleep, a miracle happens.

The idea of having the miracle happen in the middle of the night makes sure that clients move out of the "what do I have to do" mode. The miracle happens without their active contribution. It is an invitation to relax instead of doing more or trying harder. The miracle is an invitation simply to enjoy and explore curiously whatever they find on the other side of the bridge.

In our experience, a careful packaging of the gift ensures that you can use the miracle question even with skeptical clients.

. . .

The pauses. Gently leave the client enough time to cross the bridge and let the miracle do its work. Especially when the miracle happens, it is important to allow enough time. Silent pauses are the best part of coaching. You are paid for doing nothing. By doing that, you are worth every cent of your fee, because when the coach does not do anything at this point, the client gains valuable time for reflection. We understand silences and pauses as the sacred thinking time of the customer.

And the miracle is that everything that you brought to this session is solved somehow . . . just like that.

Normally it is not necessary for the coach to describe exactly what the miracle will contain. Leaving it open invites the client to construct his or her own suitable miracle.

You wake up the next morning.

It is very useful to let the miracle happen as soon as possible after the coaching session. This way, the client can start imagining a new beginning with a new perspective as soon as possible.

You do not know that there has been a miracle because you were fast asleep and nobody told you that a miracle happened.

This part of the question serves to intensify the moment of surprise. The miracle is not about anything that the client can know beforehand. It is about something that happens suddenly. Since it is part of the miracle question to invite the client to change his or her perspective, it is helpful to clarify that there is no other way of finding out anything about the miracle except by a thorough and precise observation.

Finding Differences That Make a Difference

Now that we have unwrapped several layers of the packaging of our present, it is time to concentrate on its actual content. The gift of the miracle question to the customer can be the process of finding out what he or she is really hoping for and what the desired future behind all the obstacles really looks like.

> So, when you wake up tomorrow morning, how will you start discovering that a miracle actually happened?

Often the first spontaneous reaction is, "I don't know." If you lean back and give the client some time to think about it, the first ideas about what would be different the morning after the miracle usually appear.

Sometimes clients will answer in negative terms: "I will not be afraid anymore." In order to turn this absence of something into the active presence of something different, we suggest asking what they would like instead. "When you are not afraid, what will be there instead?" This helps the client to describe the differences that arise in the form of positive actions.

> Coach: What else would be different in the morning or the day after the miracle?

In order to gain the most benefit from the miracle question, you can continue to ask "What else?" at this point. These additional moments of discovery can be positioned at several points in time later during the client's day or at other places, at home, at work, and so on. After collecting a multitude of differences, the coach may choose a few topics that seem especially helpful to the client trying to reach the goal.

Exploring Action-Based Consequences in Real Life

The central aspect of the preferred future consists of finding out which consequences the miracle will have in terms of the real-life actions of the client.

This is where the miracle question is very much down to earth and completely in the everyday reality of the customer. Our main focus during the conversation needs to be on the client and on what he or she would be doing differently as a consequence of the miracle in his or her real life. We stress the action and the doing because we believe that it is vital for clients to be clear about what they could do differently, no matter how the miracle influences their feelings and emotions.

How will your friend notice that the miracle happened to you?

Questions about the perspective of others and about what they would notice in the client automatically lead to relevant differences in observable behavior. Bosses, family members, partners, or whoever is important to the client can provide a useful outside perspective. The more detailed the preferred future picture becomes for the client, the better the chances of discovering useful ideas that can be tried out in action.

Alternatives to the Miracle Question

Sometimes practitioners feel uncomfortable talking about a miracle in a business setting. They would rather have an alternative question with a similar effect of mentally inviting the customer to move in time from before the obstacle to after the obstacle.

As a rule, we can say that the more desperate or challenging the situation of the client, when it would really take some kind of a miracle, the more effectively the original miracle question works.

Of course, there are other possibilities for exploring the preferred future and inviting the client to look beyond the obstacle.

Suppose some time has passed and consequently you have managed to reach your goal. What would you be doing differently then?

Suppose your boss suddenly behaves the way you want him to. How will that make a difference?

The language pattern of the question always starts with "Suppose . . ." Clients have all different kinds of obstacles like "we do not have enough resources" or "first the boss would need to change" that may block their way. In the middle part of constructing the question, you take whatever the client names as the obstacle and turn it into a possibility. "So let's suppose just for a moment, you had enough resources / your boss would change somehow . . ." You can even add something along the lines of "Of course there is no way of knowing if this is ever going to happen or how it will happen, so just suppose . . ." The final piece of the question can be, "What will you be doing then, that you are not doing now?" or "How will you react differently to that?"

The aim of the coach is to connect the client with everything that is waiting behind the goal. This is why it sometimes happens that the goal shifts at this point. Ms. K.'s goal in the beginning was to somehow be able to deal with her work situation. But this goal had been formulated from the perspective of trying to solve the problem. This initial perspective changed when she entered the solution-building framework by answering the miracle question. Ms. K. realized that she wanted to be respected, to be proud of herself, and to take care of herself and her resources better.

Half-Time Experiment

This experiment might take a little courage. A few years back, Peter used it in his coaching practice for 6 months to learn more about the effects of the miracle question. You can try it more safely in supervision groups if you prefer.

The self-imposed half-time rule goes like this. If the coaching session is set for 1 hour, you ask the miracle question after exactly 30 minutes. Whatever length you expect the session to be, commit yourself to asking the miracle question exactly in the middle of the conversation.

Carefully observe differences in the coaching conversation before and after the miracle question is asked. What specifically became possible before and after the miracle question?

This experiment can be helpful to learn more about which cases the miracle question is appropriate for, and what is a good time to ask it. It might be that you find the miracle question useful even when you did not expect it.

Make notes about your discoveries.

7

Finding Resources and Precursors of Solutions

This third phase of the coaching conversation is designed to strengthen the confidence of the client in the plan. Once clients are clear on what kind of life they really want to live, it is useful to find out whether their endeavors are realistic and how their goals can be reached.

Asking for Precursors

In brief coaching, we very carefully ask about examples and incidents in which the client has already experienced a little bit of the preferred future, times when something already went in the desired direction, or experiences that seemed like small moments of the ideal future in the present. These experiences usually contain a lot of valuable information about solutions.

We like to call these moments precursors of the preferred future. Once you have found such examples, you can use them to find out more about what exactly the client has contributed to make these successes possible. Once it is clear what worked in a specific moment, and clients become aware of their own resources, it is so much easier to do more of what has already proven to work.

We sometimes call this phase of the conversation the "solution surfing" phase: the client has discovered a forward-moving wave pointing exactly in the desired direction. Like a surfer in the ocean, the client can now comfortably surf on these forward-moving forces and easily make more progress.

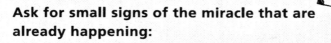

FOR YOUR TOOLKIT

Ask for small signs of the miracle that are already happening:

- What was the most recent time when you remember something happening that was at least a little bit like the miracle?
- What other examples of such precursors come to mind?
- How did you manage to do that? What did you contribute to make this possible?

Coaching in Action
Ms. K.

When I asked about small signs of the miracle that had already happened, Ms. K. described how she had come close to the miracle when she had been at the sauna a few weeks earlier and how she had gone to dinner with a former colleague two days ago.

> Coach: Oh really? I bet it wasn't easy to move out of this tired loneliness that you described. How did you manage to do that?
> Ms. K.: When I was at work, I simply had the idea that I might go to the sauna. I remember that I was very angry about something that Dr. F. had said and that I thought, enough is enough. I even went home earlier that afternoon.
> Coach: So you somehow managed to decide to take good care of yourself.

Ms. K. and I took some time in the conversation to examine these precursors of the miracle. In the process, Ms. K. started to discover that it was easier to stay calm at work and to deal with the pressure if she had taken the time to take good care of herself beforehand. This discovery led to other precursors of the

43

miracle—situations in which she had managed to take things that had not gone well less personally. Ms. K. even remembered a single small incident when Dr. F. had given her some recognition. By examining this incident, Ms. K. suddenly realized how she had contributed to this huge miracle very elegantly—and she was thrilled!

Forerunners of the miracle are
like delicate flowers growing toward
the solution in the thicket of the problem.

The more examples of precursors or glimpses of the solution can be discovered in the memory of the client, the better. Every example carries valuable information about possible actions, choices, and resources that have already been proven to work in the reality of the client.

Asking your customers about precursors is like gently inviting them to move their focus of attention from what is missing to what is already in place.

First you need to put yourself in the clients' place, seeing what they see. Acknowledge the obstacle they see in front of them and that it will not be easy to overcome. And then at some point you gently start tapping on the client's shoulder. You point in a slightly different direction and ask, "And can you tell me what you discover over there? Let's talk about what is already working well." This is an invitation of the coach to broaden the clients' perspective and to discover other portions of reality that were originally not in their focus of attention.

Valuing the Ability to Cope

A special resource that often appears when you explore precursors of the miracle and the resources connected to them is the capability of the client to cope with very difficult situations.

There are limitations in life that cannot be changed. In Ms. K.'s example, no one could even be sure whether it would be possible to improve her situation at work or whether there was actually anything that she could actively contribute to it. And surely the coach did not have any influence on the job market and Ms. K.'s chances of finding a new job. It might just have been the case that she would simply have to stay in her old job. This is also why it is appropriate to explore precursors of the miracle very thoroughly. These precursors showed how Ms. K. had been able to cope with an unchanged and very difficult situation. One of the most valuable resources in the face of such a bleak future could be doing more of what helps her "suffer the slings and arrows of outrageous fortune." Ms. K. remembered precursors that were connected to her ability to cope with this difficult situation. If she had not remembered them on her own, the coach would have reacted with a variation of the question. He would not have simply tapped on her shoulder gently but would have tapped a bit more heartily. These kinds of questions are also called coping questions: "What you are going through at the moment is unbelieveable. It's amazing that you are able to get up in the morning every day and go to work in spite of all these difficulties. I'm really asking myself, how do you manage to do that?"

FOR YOUR TOOLKIT

Coping questions:

- How do you cope with the situation?
- How do you find the confidence and hope to go on?

Complimenting Resources

In this paragraph, we are looking at helping customers gain confidence and trust in the feasibility of what they want to achieve.

Discovering unexpected strengths of our customers is something that really helps. All of our coaching clients demonstrate personal qualities and experiences that can be very useful for mastering the challenges they are facing. These qualities or resources—resilience in difficult times, the ability to work hard, a sense of humor, the willingness to listen to others and to help, being able to establish precise projects and plans, an interest in learning—are a useful basis for creating change.

Compliments need to be authentic and should not be used as a manipulative communication trick. You should not use compliments if you just want to be friendly or nice. In such cases, you lose credibility quickly. Helpful compliments are founded on real incidents and arise out of what the conversation partner communicates verbally or by his or her behavior.

Compliments are very powerful coaching tools. They support hope and confidence for the next steps in the development of the client. They also shed light on past strengths and successes, which may also be helpful for reaching the client's goals.

You probably know about this from your own experience. Which compliments do you still remember from your childhood or adolescence? Most often these compliments are still part of how you look at yourself. They might even have had an influence on your profession today.

So do take time as a coach to give compliments about what impresses you. You thereby strengthen the confidence and trust of the client. In our experience, the most effective reinforcement for the customer that you as a coach can give is to ask your clients to talk about what they are proud of and then reinforce these statements with honest compliments.

Coaching in Action:
Finding a Focus in Complex Situations

At this point, Ms. K. was both confident and curious. Therefore, it seemed appropriate to focus on what she had just rediscovered about herself and anchor what was working well and the other useful resources connected to it.

> Coach: Let me ask you another somewhat strange question based on what you just said. Take a scale from 1 to 10. One on the scale is the moment in which you were first confronted with the reorganization in your job, and 10 is the morning after the miracle. Where are you now on the scale?

Ms. K. said that she was already on a 3. I asked her to summarize the differences between her current 3 and the initial 1. Together we collected things that had been helpful to get from 1 to 3.

> Coach: Where were the things that you just talked about—the sauna, the dinner, and the recognition by Dr. F.—on the same scale of 1 to 10?
>
> Ms. K.: The dinner was at a 6, the sauna at 7 because I decided to go there by myself. Getting Dr. F. to praise me was clearly a 9.

Scaling Questions

Scaling questions are wonderful and easy-to-use tools that help to construct an overall picture of the progress that has been achieved. Customers often tell us that scaling helps them to visualize the distance that they have already covered. It is also helpful to remember that there were times when they were able to reach a much higher number on the scale.

When they become aware of some actual examples that are higher on the scale, our clients' confidence also rises: "If I have already been able to do this once, there is a realistic chance that I will be able to continue doing it or doing more of it."

In brief coaching, we assume that it is much easier for people to base changes on something that has already worked. This strategy tends to be quite successful. We don't think that clients should learn something completely new, or that they have to change their ways completely in order to reach their goals. On the contrary, we are convinced that it is much more useful to rediscover existing resources and use them.

Scaling questions 1:

- On a scale of 1 to 10, which describes the progress that you want to make? Where would you say you are at the moment?

- What is different now if you compare it to when you were at a 1?

- What helped you to get from a 1 to where you are now?
- Where were the examples that you described as precursors of the solution or exceptions on the same scale?
- What would your best friend say about where you are on the scale? What would he or she admire about your progress?

EXPERIMENT

Diary of Taking Good Care of Myself

We designed this diary experiment for the participants in our coaching training workshops. It has proven to be helpful for the quick and easy development of coaching competencies.

We don't know how you do it—you probably only look at what you are happy with and what works well in your coaching so that you can learn from these resources.

However, we noticed that some of the participants in our workshops seem to observe the opposite—all the things that they did "wrong." This is why we created a little diary that we hand out to the workshop participants on the first evening of their coaching course. It is simply an ordinary diary that is available everywhere. One difference, however, is a small sticker that says: "Diary of taking good care of myself." We take a lot of time to explain to the participants that this is no usual diary but that we have invested years of research together with the paper industry to develop a very special and unusual kind of paper. The upper layer of the paper has been treated in such a way that it will only make those entries visible that describe resources, precursors, and positively stated goals and next small steps. Therefore, there is actually no way to enter information about your own deficits, obstacles, or things that didn't work well. These entries simply don't show on the paper.

The participants then are given time each evening to reflect on their learning in this special way and to take notes in their diary.

If you think that this could be a helpful learning experience for yourself, we suggest that you also acquire such a diary. It might be difficult to find a shop that will have our special diaries in stock. So if your local store does not have such a diary, don't hesitate to simply buy one that you like and then pretend that it is one of these special diaries. Just act as if this was the kind of paper that only allows entries that reflect your taking good care of yourself when you are writing on it.

Defining Progress Clues

In a typical brief coaching session, after exploring the preferred future as well as the resources of the client, the next element of the conversation is geared toward increasing the chances of concrete action-based steps toward the goal.

A few years ago, we met Sir Edmund Hillary at a conference about leadership. He was one of the first people to set foot on the summit of Mount Everest. Sir Edmund was talking about the qualities of leadership necessary to be successful in doing something nobody had done before. He said that what he and his Sherpa, Tenzing Norgay, had done would nowadays seem ridiculous and amateurish from the viewpoint of a modern professional mountaineer. "We had very simple equipment and very primitive climbing techniques. The only thing that we really knew how to do well was carving one step after the other into the snow. In all humility I can say that we were champions in simply shaping and preparing the next step in the snow or ice, which then got us one step closer to our goal."

Asking for Signs of Upcoming Progress

Sir Edmund was obviously very clear about his clues for upcoming progress on his journey. In brief coaching it is important to make sure that your clients have clues for their upcoming progress and some clear ideas on how to take a doable next step toward the goal in the reality of their world.

A caterpillar cannot reach its potential by taking flying lessons but only by its development into a butterfly.

Coaching in Action:
Small Steps With Ms. K.

Since we had already worked with scaling questions in this coaching, it was quite easy to continue working with scaling.

I said, "Ms. K., on a scale of 1 to 10, you just said that you were now at a 3. How will you notice that you are one step ahead, that you have moved from a 3 to a 4?"

She said that she would surely know that she was one step ahead if she answered job advertisements with more self-confidence and hope. If she was more self-confident, she would only respond to advertisements that seemed attractive to her and that were for positions in which she would be able to contribute a lot of her experience and resources. She would stop sending out applications without really being interested only because she was afraid that she wouldn't find anything better. She would remember to remind herself of times when she had received appreciation for her work when she was writing an application. This would then enable her to write with a feeling of dignity, humility, and pride.

She would also be one step higher on the scale if she felt fresh enough to go out after work at least once a week. She wasn't sure how she would notice that she was one step ahead at work. She thought that she might have developed a healthy detachment and that she would possibly be able to sit a little bit straighter on her chair. Possibly she would even lean back a little bit to create a small safety distance, something like an airbag, if there were confrontations between her and her superiors.

> Coach: I am impressed by how clear you are about the physical differences that will tell you that you're one step higher on your scale. Which of these points would be most useful to elaborate?
>
> Ms. K.: Probably the airbag situation. I would really like to know how I can behave differently during long working days so that they are healthier for me.
>
> Coach: Okay, let's have a look at the things that you would notice, things that you would be doing differently if you had the airbag. What would be a small step in this direction?

Beginnings are imbued with magic.
—Herman Hesse

FOR YOUR TOOLKIT

Asking for signs of upcoming progress:

- How will you notice that you are a small step higher on the scale?

$$1 \overline{\qquad \times \overset{+1}{\qquad}} 10$$

- How would other people in your environment notice?
- What would you do then that you are not yet doing now?
- When you leave this room, what would be a first small sign that you are on your way up the scale? What else?
- Suppose you could stay one step higher on the scale over the next few days. How would that make a difference? How would you react differently?

Using Language Effectively

There are many ways of asking clients for their next small steps. We would like to invite you to have a close look at how language is used here. If you become aware of the many options to formulate questions, you will also increase your repertoire for being helpful as a coach.

Brief coaches often ask how clients will notice that they are one step higher on the scale. This is different from asking, "What do you need to do to get one step higher?" The second question is about figuring out how to get there and start designing forward-moving actions. Asking about how clients will notice is pointing toward something completely different. Presupposing that progress will happen anyway, the aim of the coach is to make sure clients know what signs of progress to look for and to attribute them to their own behavior when they happen.

Our British colleague Harry Norman told us about a customer who was almost offended when he was asked, "So what do you need to do to get one step ahead?" The customer answered, "Do you think I'm stupid? Do you really think I would be sitting here in this coaching session if I had an answer to that question? That's your job!"

Harry apologized immediately and asked if he could ask another question. The customer agreed and Harry asked the following: "How would you notice that you're one step ahead?"

The customer smiled and said, "You're right. This is a question that only I can answer."

When clients start to observe themselves differently and start to notice what works, they are more in touch with their own existing resources and their own useful behavior. In our experience, change happens fast and sustainably this way.

The Importance of Being Small

Coaching in Action:
A Timber Mill in Canada (from our colleague Alan Kay in Toronto)

There were two teams in a timber company that were being coached in a solution-focused way: the sales department in Toronto and the production department, which was 500 miles north in the middle of the woods in Canada. Both teams were having conflicts because production planning often did not match the specifications of the customers. This was not an easy task. There were often unconstructive conversations of this kind: "I told you that the customer wanted it this way!" The answer was: "No, you didn't tell us, and by the way we can't do it this week anyway." There were threats to close down the timber mill if the sales figures continued to go down. This would have meant an economic disaster in the city in which the timber mill was located because most people there worked for the timber mill. The two teams met and found out—much to their surprise—that they had a lot in common. They had also worked well together in the past when it had become necessary.

The question that Alan asked at the end of the coaching session was, "Think about a few simple things that you might do differently. Of those things, what would most likely happen first on Monday morning? Please take care to change as little as possible."

A group of salespeople and production people agreed to have a teleconference in order to adapt the ordering form and especially the instructions for delivery. This was one of the four small tasks that they set for themselves for Monday and the following days.

One year later, the timber town had been successfully saved. Asked about how they had managed to do that, the customer said, "In the end, it was really the sum of all the small steps that made a big difference."

We want to emphasize that it is important to keep changes small. We all remember meetings in which we suddenly start enthusiastically discussing great things that need to be done—and a few days later we all feel overwhelmed by our daily routines and find no time to start large

Small changes can have large effects in a system. So it's better to make small, realistic, humble, and therefore feasible plans.

projects. It is much more likely for ideas to be implemented if they are embedded in daily activities and you can start right away, because "all beginnings are about making a beginning."

Talking about small steps often also decreases the pressure on the customer. Often clients are already under a lot of pressure: For example, people who are looking for a job, or who would like to improve their time management. It is helpful for them to ask for small steps that reduce the unproductive pressure ("I have been doing everything all wrong! It will be very strenuous to take this next large step!") and thereby increase the likelihood of first small successes.

Coaching in Action:
Concrete Actions With Ms. K.

Ms. K. wanted to elaborate her new idea of the "airbag" some more.

Ms. K.: I think I would sometimes like to care less. It's not about not caring at all, because I do want to do my job well, but maybe I could care less about things that I cannot change.

Coach: Doing your job well seems really important to you. And how could you still do a step in the right direction?

Ms. K.: Last Tuesday, for example, Dr. F. came in and threw a pile of reports onto my desk, saying that they would have to be done immediately. I couldn't help it—I had to cry when he left. This was simply too much. There is no way I can satisfy both superiors! Dr. W. had also given me an urgent task to be done immediately. They can't expect me to do everything at once!

Coach: I see that this is not easy for you. So how would you act differently if you had this airbag that you talked about?

Ms. K.: Then I would probably tell myself that the only thing that I can do is to do my best.

Coach: Suppose you told yourself that. What difference would it make?

Ms. K.: I would be much more relaxed.

Coach: Let's say you tell yourself, "I will simply do the best I can" and you are more relaxed. What would you do differently then?

Ms. K.: You know what? I would probably take a short break and get myself a cup of coffee before starting anything else.

Coach: So you take a short break . . . I understand. So Dr. F. puts his report on your table and . . .

Ms. K.: Yes, I think it would be most important to get out as soon as he left. This way I wouldn't be stuck behind my desk. I probably still don't know what I should tell Dr. F., but it's okay. First I have to get up and move. And then I would take time to choose what I should start doing next. That way I know that I am doing my best. And maybe I will also think about our conversation and will remember that it is really about taking good care of myself and gaining a safe distance.

Coach: So these would be clear signs that you have installed your safety airbag well. What else would tell you in the course of the day that you are well on your way toward the next small steps?

After a few additional detailed descriptions of the next step, I asked Ms. K. if there was anything else that we should look at that day. However, that was not the case.

In business and management contexts, we are used to finishing meetings by converting options into a clear action plan consisting of several points. We know that clearly formulated results, well-distributed roles and responsibilities, and exact deadlines help achieve something.

Many coaches ask their clients to mail them a summary of the session within 24 hours and to write down the actions that they have decided to tackle. And sometimes clients even send an e-mail 24 hours before the next session in which they describe what they have achieved.

> *Always act to increase*
> *the number of choices.*
> *—Heinz von Foerster*

Supporting clients effectively in the implementation of their plans is one of the core coaching competencies defined by the International Coach Federation. One very respectful way of offering support and continuing to view the customer as expert for his or her own solution is to ask, "How can I support you in taking responsibility for what you have decided to do?"

Increasing Choice

Since this is a book about brief coaching, we would like to offer you a different perspective for dealing with next small steps. The above-mentioned options probably work very well to make sure that small steps really happen. Brief coaches prefer to open up the wide field of possible action ideas without committing the customer to one or more specific actions. The attitude of the coach is to trust in the fact that the client will choose the option that fits best with a given situation and that these choices cannot always be planned and foreseen. Rather, we expect an emergent process where the best-fitting option might only show up along the way.

Creating a large number of choices instead of limiting them to a few is helpful, especially when you think about keeping coaching brief and effective. On the one hand, it is the role of the coach to provide the best possible beginning of something new: the more choices that are available, the more likely one of them will fit. On the other hand, you can never know whether the client will return for another session. If you encourage your customer to concentrate on a limited number of possibilities, it is likely that what looked quite promising in the beginning does not fit the reality of life. In long-term coaching it is not as important to open up choice because you can use the next session to think about new options if the agreed one does not work. However if you work with the end in mind, as in brief coaching, there are good reasons to keep the choices as manifold and as open as possible in order to increase the chances of success for the client.

EXPERIMENT

This is also an experiment that was designed for our coaching students. You probably know the feeling right at the end of an inspiring training course. You are full of good new ideas and full of good intentions eager to try them out back in the real world.

This prediction task is reportedly extremely helpful for putting learning into action.

Prepare a sheet of paper with the following structure:

Date	Prediction: Will I get a chance to try out something new today?	Points
Day 1		
Day 2		
Etc. to Day 10		

Take 10 seconds at the beginning of each day to look at your schedule. Then make a prediction, yes or no, about whether there will be a chance or not for you to try out some of the new ideas you discovered in this book. Of course, there is no way of really knowing what situations will emerge in your conversations with other people during the coming day. So you have to take a guess. Write your prediction on the list and check back at the end of the day. You get points for correct predictions. Continue the experiment for the next 10 days with the exception of 3 free days with no obligation to make a prediction. You can get a maximum of 7 points for the 7 days. How many points do you think you will make out of the 7?

In our courses, we explain to participants how they can cheat a bit to make more points. If you predict yes and no chances pop up until the end of the day, you could act as if the last person you meet in your office looks like he or she really needs a miracle. So you get to ask the miracle question and win a point. On the other hand, if you predict no and a client obviously creates a perfect opportunity for you, ignore it. Do what you used to do before in such situations and win a point.

As you might already suspect (or notice when you do it), this experiment is carefully designed to take pressure off while at the same increasing the chances of noticing good opportunities for putting what you learned into practice.

Coming to a
Session Conclusion

If you know that your first session might be the only one that you and your client are going to have, you want to provide the best possible conclusion as a preparation for life after the coaching. Naturally, there can be good reasons for agreeing on a second or third session if your client asks for it. However, it is important in brief coaching to make sure that you know when and how to say goodbye.

Planning the Last Minutes

Some minutes before the end of the coaching session, you can start thinking about the following options.

FOR YOUR TOOLKIT

Hints for Closing a Brief Coaching Session

Open Topics
- Before we end our conversation today, is there anything we forgot to talk about?
- How can we best close the session to bring it to a complete end for you?

Rechecking the Goal

- In relation to your goals for this session, where do you stand on a scale of 1 to 10? Can we leave it at that for now?

Thinking Break

This is a good time to carefully select a few reinforcing compliments and maybe think about an experiment task for the client.

- At this point I would like to take a short break to think about what I heard from you. I will leave you for a moment. You can just relax. When I come back, I will let you know what went through my head.

Compliment/Feed-forward

- Thinking about the things you said, I am really impressed by . . .

Experiment Tasks

- I have this idea for an experiment, which you might want to try out and which might support you reaching your goal . . .

Agreeing on a Next Session

- How should we proceed? Of course you are welcome to call me anytime if you want a follow-up session. Some of my clients prefer to set a fixed date for a next session. Others prefer to find out how things work out in real life first. Just let me know what suits you best.

> *The conclusion of a coaching conversation is a very good time to name all the clients' competencies and resources that give us confidence that they will reach their goal.*
> *There are generally a lot of resources that we can hand over to our clients in all appreciation like a beautiful bunch of flowers.*

Some of the above points are clear and obvious. In our training sessions, we take some more time for two of these points: compliments and experiments. There is remarkable research on both areas that warrants a closer look.

Appreciative Reinforcement

Compliments or appreciative reinforcement are always high up on the list in surveys about what coaches did in the coaching session that was most helpful for clients.

Compliments seem to provide a good opportunity to support clients on their way to their goals. This is why we always close the coaching conversation with a few sentences starting with "I am impressed . . .". We then say what our client is especially good at, or we mention actions of the client that seem especially helpful for reaching that goal.

Naturally, compliments are not restricted to the end of the session. There are many things that you automatically do during the session that show your appreciation to your client. Merely the fact that you are interested in the client and that you direct all your curiosity and attention to how the client is able to manage his or her life makes a big difference.

Timothy Gallway said, "As a coach, I believe in what I don't see." This is a way of looking at clients, the belief in their potential and abilities even if you cannot really see them as fully developed yet. Noticing resources that are there even though you cannot see them is probably one of the biggest compliments.

Seeing with the special eyes of the coach and trusting in the potential of the customer, as well as the process of working together, is what giving appreciative reinforcement is all about.

Suggestions for Experiments

Suggesting homework or an experiment to clients can support them sustainably on their way to the goal. Especially in brief coaching, experiments are important because you only see the client a few times. It is therefore even more relevant to make sure that the surfing wave that rose up in the coaching session will also support the client between sessions. A scientific study has shown that experiment tasks are helpful in significantly reducing the number of necessary sessions.[*]

	Success Rate	Number of Sessions
With experiment	86 %	2.9
Without experiment	86 %	4.2

If something works, do more of it. If something doesn't work, do something different.

The basic rules for experiments are very simple. The first rule is actually a warning to the coach: "Don't fix what is not broken!" Natu-

---

[*] The study was conducted at the BFTC on Brief Therapy sessions.

rally, it is our customers who can assess what is broken. If it's not a problem for your customer, don't mess with it as a coach.

The second rule is just as clear: If what the customer does works, encourage him or her to do more of it. A large part of brief coaching consists of a conversation about what works anyway. This is why it is very simple for clients to do more of what works—this is almost like an implicit homework assignment they give themselves. Making compliments about the helpful things clients are already doing reinforces this process and you do not need additional suggestions for experiments.

The third rule says: If a client does something that doesn't work, encourage him or her to do something different. There is an alternative to this rule, which does not seem very helpful to us. It says: "Try harder!" Do more of what doesn't work, but do it more intensively. We all know the admonitions of others: It didn't work because you didn't try hard enough. If at first you don't succeed, try, try again! Let's take the example of an employee who has already tried three times to convince his boss that he needs a raise. What will be his chances for success if he tries it for a fourth time and uses the same arguments? If he nags for a fourth time? When we say, do something different, we mean doing something that is really different. Clients most often know best what would be really different. If you ask them what they could do that would be the biggest surprise in their environment, they most often come up with a lot of very helpful ideas quickly.

Doing Something Different

In brief coaching, there are three typical suggestions for homework of the type "doing something different."

Observation Experiment

Doing something different is already built into the observation experiment. The client has probably already observed a lot of things before he or she came to coaching. Usually these observations are about what is going wrong and what led to the difficulties the client is in. Our suggestion to our customer is to do something different, namely, observing what is working and how it is working. The client is confronted with a reality that is so large that he or she can always only perceive a part of it (for example, that there is someone who is constantly nagging). We invite our customers to perceive another part of reality (for example, the fact that he is sometimes surprisingly nice). Part of the coaching time is used to practice this kind of solution-focused observation with the client.

Pretending Experiment

The pretending experiment is not about changing the observation, but about introducing a small difference when you are in the middle of things. The customer is invited to pretend that the miracle already happened. For the outside world, this might just look like the client is really doing something different even though he or she is just pretending. The more time that is spent during the coaching conversation drawing a detailed picture of the morning after the miracle, the easier it becomes for the client to pretend that the miracle has already happened. The experiment is limited in time (e.g., an hour during the day) so that clients have enough opportunity to observe useful differences in themselves or others.

Prediction Experiment

The prediction experiment introduces doing something different on yet another level. The customer is invited to change the focus of his or her attention from doing something right to predicting correctly whether it will happen or not. Some customers feel an increasing pressure to produce the right results and appropriate performance, and putting more pressure on them would be less than helpful. The prediction experiment is about making a different kind of effort. Customers get points when they predict the unpredictable correctly—and that takes a lot of pressure off them. (For example, is he going to nag or not, independently of what I am doing?)

Suggestions For experiments

Choose one of the three possibilities.

Presentation for all three experiments: "I had an idea about something that might help you reach your goal. Of course, there are no guarantees, but it only takes little or no additional time. Would you like to hear what it's about?"

Observation Experiment

"During the next days, please observe carefully what happens that is okay the way it is, and what things you would like to have more of. Hopefully, this kind of information will somehow be useful for you to reach your goal. Maybe you would also like to make notes and tell me about what happened in the next session."

Pretending Experiment

"Select a few days or hours in the next week in which you will pretend that it is the morning after the miracle. Today you described in various ways what would be different then and how you would react differently. Keep it secret and tell nobody that you are pretending. Just observe carefully how other people react so that we can talk about it next time."

Prediction Experiment

"I would like to invite you to try to predict every evening from now on until our next conversation whether the thing we talked about will happen the next day or not. Naturally, you can neither know nor really influence it. Just guess and determine the next evening whether you were right. Every correct prediction will give you a point and the next time, you can tell me how many points you've gotten."

Coaching in Action:
Thinking Break for Ms. K.

During the thinking break that I took during the coaching session with Ms. K., it became clear to me very quickly which kind of compliment I would like to give her. I was very impressed at how she was able to manage go to work every morning despite all the trouble and still take care of herself although she was dealing with what other people would probably call an unbearable work situation. She had managed to get from a 1 to a 3 and even had moments of 6, 7, and 9. Finding an experiment or homework for her needed a little bit more time. She seemed to have several goals. One was finding a new position and increasing her self-confidence; another was being able to bear the unbearable situation at her current job better and taking good care of herself. In the end I had three ideas, one for each form of experiment.

The observation was very easy. She should direct her attention to the moments in which she was taking good care of herself.

The pretending was a little bit more tricky. I had no doubt that she was able to pretend the miracle had happened when she was at home. But I wasn't so sure whether it wouldn't be asking too much of her to try this at work. In this kind of experiment, she would need the freedom to choose whether to pretend that the miracle happened for an hour at work or for an hour at home.

The prediction was easy. After she discovered that she did have a little bit of influence on Dr. F., she would be able to predict whether he would give her a compliment the next day or not.

In the end, I decided on the simplest and easiest variant: the observation experiment. I invited Ms. K. to buy an attractive diary for taking good care of herself and to enter everything that made her a little bit proud of herself. I hoped she would be able to bear the situation at her workplace a little better if she realized when she was taking good care of herself during the day. Maybe she could also gain enough self-confidence to be able to successfully apply for new positions.

Designing the experiment and packaging it well is a lot of fun. However, it is clients who should decide whether they would like to try one of the suggested experiments. Coachees have very good intuition about what is most helpful for them.

All Your Work-Related Problems Are Solved

This is a task that Insoo Kim Berg liked to give participants at the end of the first workshop day. You should also be able to try this experiment at the end of any day quite easily. Insoo told the participants that they should pretend that the door to the workshop room had a kind of invisible miracle shower built in. "The effect of this miracle shower is that all the problems that you have at work have been solved, just like in the miracle. Therefore, it is your task to go through the door and pretend that the miracle happened from the moment that you exit this room until you enter it again the next morning. Observe carefully how you react differently in the evening, at home or wherever you are going. Observe also how other people around you react differently. And don't tell anybody that you are doing this task—simply observe carefully what is different. We will talk about it tomorrow morning."

When the participants came back the next day, Insoo invited them to pair up and ask one another how they noticed that the miracle happened and what other people noticed that was different with them. Typically there were some participants who reluctantly admitted that they had forgotten to do the homework. Insoo simply said, "Oh really? Don't worry. Just pretend that you did the homework and tell the other person what you would have noticed, had you done the homework."

10

Follow-up Sessions

Whenever clients do come back for a follow-up session, the main focus of attention should be finding out about improvements, about how they were achieved, and about how they can be maintained.

If you want something to grow,
you have to recognize small
signs and care for them just
like you care for a sprouting plant.

Asking What Has Become Better

In brief coaching, most follow-up sessions start with the question "What is better?" This serves to direct the attention of the client to what is already working well and is pointing in the right direction. We want to focus on what the client has done to get closer to the goal. We are curious and ask for a certain kind of events and memories from the multitude of things that happened to the client between sessions.

This is a bit like the gardener in the movie *Being There* who is looking after the flowers in the garden. There is also a birch tree that has obviously lost some leaves, which are now lying on the ground, and maybe the buds of his favorite rosebush are gone because some children picked them. However, the rest of the flowers look somewhat like they did before. But then there are also some promising new buds in a flowerbed. If you want something to grow, you have to recognize small signs and care for them like you care for a new sprout. You have to look carefully if you want to find them. You have search your memory, identify small differences, and select those that signify progress. And suddenly when you have identified the first detail of progress, you notice that there is much more proof of growth around you than you might have initially expected.

Customers don't usually look for what has become better since the last session. It seems as if human communication was invented mainly in order to complain. Of course, that is quite okay and can be a lot of fun, too. Our colleague from Vienna, Sonja Radatz, says that the inhabitants of the city of Sigmund Freud have cultivated complaining as an art form. If there is nothing to complain about, it can't be fun. And even though—or because—we know that and accept it, it is our task as coaches to offer the opportunity to spend the coaching session doing something even more useful than complaining.

You should expect that the answer to the question "what is better?" will require some serious thinking on the part of the client before he or she can truly respond to the question. The most frequent answer that you will hear is either "I don't know" or "nothing." Often this is just another way of saying, "Oh, I have never thought about this. Please give me some more time to think." So as a coach, just sit back quietly and give your customer some time for the search process.

Coaching in Action:
Self-coaching on the Bicycle

I remember a customer who was an especially intelligent and dynamic young man. He was head of the welfare department of his city and came for his third coaching session. As usual, I first asked him whether there was a special topic for which we should reserve some time in the coaching session. He said that there was an important board meeting that he would like to prepare for during the session. We agreed to do that in a few minutes. Then I asked my formal beginning question for follow-up sessions, maybe exactly like I had asked it a few weeks before when he had arrived for his second session: "Can you tell me what has been better since we last met?" The young man looked at me and started smiling broadly. "I knew it—I simply knew that you would ask me this question today! This is why I already prepared for it on my way here when I was riding my bicycle. So . . ."

This was the first time I realized why brief coaching tends to be so short. It uses very simple coaching procedures, and clients learn very quickly. They learn so quickly that they only need a few sessions to increase their ability to usefully focus their awareness. If I remember correctly, this third session was either our last session or the next to last. This was a really intelligent young man, and he therefore learned very quickly anyway.

FOR YOUR TOOLKIT

Questions for following sessions:

- Are there any special issues for which we should plan some time today?

Questions about the time between conversations:

- What is better?
- And what else is better?
- How did you manage to do that? What did you contribute?
- What would other people say has become better?
- What else would they say?
- Where are you now on a scale of 1 to 10?
- What could I see that you're doing now that you weren't doing before?
- How can you support yourself in keeping up these changes?

71

Coaching in Action:
Ms. K.: A New Job at 55

When Ms. K. called 3 weeks later, I was a bit reluctant to ask what was better. Her description of the difficult situation in her work and life was still very vivid in my memory. I had thought that we would probably need a miracle to make something better. However, much to my surprise, it was relatively easy for her to answer my question. Ms. K. said that her biggest improvement was that she was increasingly able to tolerate the situation at her workplace. She had become so good at it that she could even imagine keeping this position and somehow get along with Dr. F. and Dr. W. She said it felt like she had rid herself of a big burden. What she was enjoying most, however, was that she now really had the choice to stay or leave. Both options were feasible.

I said, "I am really very impressed and relieved to hear that, Ms. K., and if I may, I would like to come back to that in a minute. Can you tell me what else has been better in the last 3 weeks?"

Ms. K. said that she had really fallen in love with her little diary about taking good care of herself and that she was now proud of a lot of things that she had entered into the little booklet. She was so proud that she had even read out some passages to her closest friends.

This reminded her of something else that had become better. Her social life was much more active. She had gone out with friends at least once a week, sometimes even on work days.

And finally, she had seen a job advertisement that was very interesting. She had mustered all her courage and called to ask a few questions and find out more about the job. She had written an application and was now waiting for the answer. But, looking at how it was at her current job, she wasn't really under a lot of pressure to find something new. She would rather carefully choose once given the opportunity.

The first minutes of the coaching session serve to provide a general overview of the various areas of improvement in the client's life. Use the drive and energy of a successful search process and try to find out what else has become better. As long as the client is in this productive mode and recalls all the things that promise hope and confidence, there is no need for the coach to interrupt. After the whole collection has been presented, it is much easier to select the incidents that are most useful to look at more closely.

Coach: Of all the things that have become better, what are you most proud of?

Ms. K.: Probably I am most proud of the way Dr. F. and Dr. W. are treating me now—as a competent and valuable person.

Coach: They do that?

Ms. K.: Dr. F. even stuck a Post-it note saying "Thank you" on my desk when I had finished a report for him after 5 o'clock. Dr. W. is much more polite and even says hello in the morning. He also asked me how I managed to work for two superiors. And I made a suggestion about how we could organize incoming work more effectively.

Coach: How did you manage to accomplish that? I can imagine that that wasn't easy.

Ms. K.: Actually, it was pretty easy. He simply became a lot more respectful toward me.

Coach: Oh, I see. He is more respectful now. If there was anything that you contributed to make it easier for him to be more respectful, what could your contribution have been?

Ms. K.: I think I know. It started a few weeks ago when he ran into my office. I had heard him arrive, and I remember looking him directly in the eye when he came in. It was just as if I was saying, "What is it now, young man?'" But I didn't say anything and simply waited until he started talking. This was the first time he said, "Ms. K., could you please . . . ." It was as if he knew that I wouldn't take it any longer.

Humble Clients

This brief sequence shows something that often happens: the client remarks that there has been an improvement and it seems as if this improvement only happened due to the circumstances or because other people did something. In order to coach effectively and to keep the improvement, it is useful to focus on the contribution of the client. What was helpful should preferably be something that the client can influence so that he or she can reproduce it. The magic question for this kind of humility is: "Naturally others were helpful, and what could you have possibly contributed to it?" The more details of their own contributions clients become aware of, the higher the probability that they will be able to reproduce the actions. This also increases the likelihood that they will be able to sustain their progress.

Ms. K. was now at a 6 on her progress scale. The main question that was still open was whether she wanted to use her energy to find a new position or not. She was really not sure. She wanted to wait for the answer to her first application and take it from there. We used the rest of the session to examine how Ms. K. could maintain her improvements and achieve a stable balance over the next few weeks. We also looked at what could support her during the normal ups and downs of the process. I expressed my admiration for everything that she had achieved: taking good care of herself, gaining respect as a competent employee at work, and taking the initiative to call the company with the job offer before actually writing the application.

You cannot teach anybody anything.
You can only help them to
discover it in themselves.
—Galileo Galilei

As in this case with Ms. K., over and over again we are surprised at how talented clients are at getting where they want all by themselves.

Moving up the Scale

In our workshops, participants ask often why we don't talk about what the client should do in order to move even further. Why don't we ask, "What will your steps toward further improvement look like?" When talking to participants, we are curious and ask, "What do you think— why don't we do that?" One of the very interesting answers that we once heard was, "Keeping something up that was achieved doesn't come easy. Having achieved something and merely sustaining it can be hard work. I think that as soon as keeping up the improvements no longer poses a challenge, the client will automatically take the next steps and doesn't need a coach for that. But you do need a coach to celebrate what has been achieved and to help the client do more of what works already."

We have nothing to add to this, except maybe that in fact some customers use the following sessions to formulate their steps to improvement. Of course, we go along with them since they are the real experts in knowing how to best reach their goal. But we wouldn't mention it first.

What Happens When Nothing Is Better?

A follow-up session like the one with Ms. K. is a wonderful experience for both coach and client. And it's not extraordinary if it happens this way. Some of the participants in our trainings worry, however: "What happens if nothing is better or, worse, things have even gotten worse? What can we do then?"

Coaching in Action:
Not Knowing Is the Best State for a Coach to Be In

A while ago, one of the participants in our training sessions had a funny experience. He participated in the first module of our coach training, which mainly deals with first sessions. In the meantime, one of his clients had shown up for a second session, and the only thing that our participant could remember was that he should start by asking, "What is better?" So he trusted in the process and was also very relaxed due to some recent first sessions that had gone really well. So he asked, "What is better?" and the customer said, "Better? Nothing!" The coach was flabbergasted and didn't know what to say. He pressed himself into his chair and was on the verge of saying to the customer, "I give up. You know, I'm just learning this stuff. I really don't know what to do next." But he was almost paralyzed by shock and needed a moment to figure out what to say. In the meantime, the customer realized that there was obviously no reaction to be expected from his coach. So he used the time to think, and said, "Okay, except maybe last week, there was this one incident that was better." And then he continued and reported relevant successes.

The coach, our participant, found this turn of his coaching conversation especially funny because he later learned that we recommend exactly his procedure —wait, don't know—in these situations. What he had done was perfectly useful, but he hadn't been aware of it. Not knowing happened simply by accident.

FOR YOUR TOOLKIT:

Emergency Kit

If the client says, "I don't know."
- Lean back and wait.
- Say, "Suppose you knew. What would you be able to tell me then?"

If the client says, "Nothing is better."
- Lean back and wait.
- Say, "I am sorry to hear that. I was hoping for something just a little bit better, at least for a brief moment."
- Say, "How come things have not become worse? How did you manage to keep it stable?"

If the client says, "It has become worse!"

- Say, "I did not realize how bad things must be for you. How do you still manage to deal with it all?"
- Say, "I realize there must be moments that are particularly bad for you. That makes me wonder: How is it different in moments that are simply bad?"

There is an old adage in brief coaching: No problem happens all the time. What happens the rest of the time?

Further Sessions

In our practice, we see most of our customers once or twice. Most of the time, the first conversation is enough and sometimes there is a single follow-up conversation enabling clients to decide that they no longer need to come to coaching. They are now prepared to pursue their goals on their own using their own resources.

Help is only useful if it liberates you from needing more help. Repeated help is no help. Don't talk about helping others except if you free them from the need for further help.
—Sri Nisargadatta Marharaj

Very rarely, clients look us up after a longer period of time in order to work on another issue with us. More often, they just seem to solve their problems on their own even though they judge the coaching to be so good and helpful that they refer other customers to us.

We sometimes wonder how we can explain this phenomenon. How can one or two conversations strengthen confidence and trust in one's own ability to solve problems so sustainably that our customers no longer need coaching?

One possibility is that our support process is so simple that it can be learned by customers in one conversation and then applied on their own.

"It is like a switch in your brain," one of our customers once said. "The switch enables you to change your own viewpoint whenever it is useful: from looking at what doesn't work to looking at what already works."

Another possibility is that customers do not need to come back because all we do is consistently reinforce what they already have: their own resources.

EXPERIMENT

Take an empty sheet of paper and write down at least 25 things that have become better for you since you started reading this book.

In our experience, giving a challenging high number of things to think of can inspire people and create a helpful framework. Even though it may seem crazy to want to find 25 things, the list may easily end up being even longer.

11

Brief Coaching of Executives: Three Examples

Looking back at the last chapters, you might be asking yourself, "Can it really be this simple?" This chapter offers three recent cases from our coaching practice with executives. You will see how the simple tool of scaling questions is adapted slightly in each case. All three examples are about making competencies of our customers accessible to them in a brief coaching session. As you know by now, coaching that builds on the competencies of the clients also is the kind of coaching that will produce not only quick but, more important, sustainable results.

- Example 1: An experienced manager in the consumer goods industry needs to gear up her leadership role.
- Example 2: A young industrial manager flunks a management assessment, but manages to gain the full trust of his boss within a few weeks of coaching.
- Example 3: A successful bank director faces a complex career change decision and discovers what he really wants in life.

In all three cases, there was only a single coaching session. All three customers came to deal with the issue at hand, on short notice. Before coaching the situation seemed gridlocked. However, in each conversation they managed to create viable options for action. In all three cases, the result proved sustainable in the long term—despite or perhaps just because of the brevity of the coaching.

Being brief means helping clients get a head start. Our experience with these three examples and many others show that clients then know how to carry on. So coaching can be designed to make further coaching superfluous since the customers' own competencies will still be there when the coach is not.

Case Example 1: Gearing Up the Leadership Role

Contracting

The coaching was set up with the human resources department of a consumer goods distributor. Helen, a high-level manager, was facing difficult strategic challenges under even more difficult circumstances and deserved all the support she could get. When Helen contacted me, we clarified the confidentiality of the coaching sessions as well as my fees, but did not define any number of sessions we would need. We agreed that we would end the coaching once Helen felt like she could move on alone. Since brief coaching usually generates the greatest added value in the first couple of hours of coaching, I sometimes charge double for them—and the first session is also a paid session, as we already mentioned. If the client feels that no value was added in the first session, of course, he or she does not pay anything at all.

Beginning of Session

Helen first described her situation, which was truly uncomfortable. A top-level manager had left the company. Without him, there was no longer sufficient executive support for an important strategic project she was in charge of. The members of her business unit—a few thousand people—felt increasingly insecure and energy was being wasted on unproductive rumors rather than creating value for the company.

I asked, "What should happen today to make this conversation worth your time?" Helen thought for a moment and decided to begin with her own behavior change on the job: "I really need to learn to assert myself—especially since the situation is so tough. I think I should come across much more strongly now, especially toward the CEO and the project team." We explored what would happen if she asserted herself more. It was obvious that this topic was very important for Helen and that she and others would profit greatly from an improvement. "Think of a scale from 1 to 10, where 10 means you assert yourself as much as necessary and 1 is the opposite. Can you show me a range on that scale, the range of your assertiveness during the last couple of weeks?" After careful consideration, Helen set the range between 2 and 4 on the scale. "Sometimes I manage better, but last week with the CEO, I just wasn't demanding and clear enough and one of my key points simply disappeared." Like many clients, Helen first looked at the moment in which she had not been able to act as she had wanted; she was focusing on her presumed deficit rather than on where she would be able to find precursors of the solution. Therefore, I became curious about how to shed some light in the opposite direction: the capabilities that she was not seeing at the moment.

"What are you already doing between 2 and 4 that you were not doing at 1?" Helen described several changes that she had successfully introduced during the last couple of weeks. For example, she had consciously started focusing on fewer priorities and had actually managed to stop doing other things. She had cancelled her attendance at a management event, and gave an internal customer the choice to decide which of two projects would temporarily be postponed. We briefly discussed how she had managed to make such clear decisions and stick to them despite the difficulties.

Goals

Helen did not want to be stuck at 2 or 4—her target was to reach at least 7 or 8 on the scale. I really liked Helen's drive and was curious to explore how much she already knew about her desired future behavior. "Let's assume you have somehow made it to 7 or 8. I also don't know right now whether that's possible or how you will manage it—

but just imagine that you are already at 7 or 8. What would you be doing differently at 7 or 8? Can you give me a few concrete things?" In the following 10 minutes, Helen developed a very detailed and multi-layered picture of the desired changes in her own behavior. I asked her how project team members would notice this, how the CEO would notice in her next contact with him, and what the first thing would be that would attract the attention of her closest coworkers when she reached 7 or 8 on the scale. We discussed too how the respective partners would probably react in conversation, and which positive effects this might have for the company.

At this point, we both knew very well that we were speaking of pure hypotheses; Helen still was between 2 and 4 on her scale. Nonetheless, the scenario of 7 or 8 seemed attractive to her and somehow I could see her determination to get there grow stronger and stronger. She was now perfectly clear on what she wanted to achieve.

More Resources

As I was listening to Helen's description of her behavior at a 7 or 8, I suspected that she must have already had some strong precursors of her goal at times when she had already been higher than 4. "Helen, what recent examples can you think of, where you showed the first signs of being closer to a 7 or 8, at least for a short while in your own behavior?" Helen thought of three examples. A situation with the CEO that she had described was somewhere around 6; another example from a departmental meeting was at 7; and a further example with the project team was also somewhere around 6. "Yes, in the last project meeting I really did react differently. We had one of these endless discussions, and I didn't let it go on. I just made a decision. I honestly admit I was somewhat annoyed in that situation, but then I surprised myself at how easily the decision was accepted and productively implemented." Exploring the successful example with the CEO (at 6 on the scale) Helen gained valuable hints about what she could do more of in order to get a clear commitment from the boss.

Wrapping Up

Based on the success factors Helen identified in the three successful examples, she drafted an action plan for her concrete steps of change within the next 72 hours: "It is entirely clear to me now what I will do more of." I was really happy for her—doing more of what works is much easier than doing something completely new or different. With a final look at her target scale, Helen remarked with some surprise, "I have already come much closer to my goal than I would have thought possible even this morning!" We concluded the session without making another appointment.

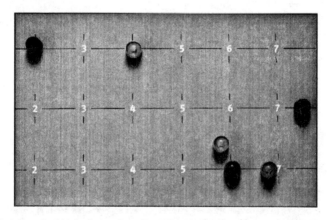

Skaleboard of Helen's session. First line: initial competency assessment between 2 and 4. Second line: goal statement at 7.5. Third line: forerunners within the last weeks between 6 and 7. Skaleboard is a magnetic coaching tool available at www.solutionsurfers.com.

Later on, I received two brief e-mails from Helen. Her more assertive behavior seemed to bear fruit. Also, she accepted an even more challenging job offer and was taking the next step in her career. The coaching had been simple. Some gentle but insistent questions reminding the client to look in the direction of her capabilities had been enough.

Case Example 2: Influencing the Boss

In some cases, executives (just like other people) want somebody else to change. This was the coaching challenge in the second case.

"In a workshop for the extended management team, we all filled in a personal DISC profile (see www.discprofile.com). In the item I for interaction/influence, I had a value of around 30, while my colleagues had values around 70. I want to get to 70, because for success in my job that would be really important. Most of all, I need to influence my boss so that he gets to trust me much more than he does now. I constantly notice that he does not really have confidence in me. He doesn't give me full responsibility, micromanages, and so on. But how can he expect me to perform, if he doesn't give me advance trust?" This is a brief summary of the concerns of a 38-year-old industrial manager named John at the beginning of our coaching session.

Competencies of Action

We started looking for resources and precursors of John's preferred future (influencing the boss to trust him). However, this proved more difficult than usual. The boss seemed to be a tough case. There seemed to be no examples of even the slightest trust. So I asked, "Tell me about your career so far. How did you manage to move up in the hierarchy so quickly? You are 38, aren't you?" He did manage identify some of his own related competencies. There had been significant examples throughout his career where he had been able to interact and influence superiors successfully. Five years ago, for example, he was given responsibility for the renovation of an entire production facility and was subsequently promoted to his current position based on this success. I could see John's animation and energy when he told me how he had gained the trust of his former bosses back then. Thanks to this recovered memory, John came up with a number of his own success factors from earlier on. Then he even remembered one situation that had actually worked with his current boss. The boss had sent him to Asia to resolve an ongoing conflict situation in one of the local branches. Now John clearly remembered how he had surprised his boss with a comment that had led to the assignment and a free hand in it. He was particularly happy about the fact that he discovered ways of exercising influence that felt authentic to him and suited him well, and that had worked before.

Competencies of Observation

Nevertheless, John still was a bit anxious and skeptical. He did not know whether his boss would really react positively when he tried out the new (and old) behavior. Would his boss really start to trust him more? Would he stop micromanaging? We both knew that our coaching session could not change his boss. However, we both agreed John would not want to miss even the smallest signs of improvement on his boss's side. Until now, John had primarily noticed when the boss yet again demonstrated no trust. It would be all the more important to notice also when the boss for once demonstrated the first small signs of extended trust.

"Let's assume that in reaction to your successful efforts your boss would really start to behave differently. How would you recognize the first positive signs of him actually trusting you?" I asked. I did not back off until John named a number of clues that he could look for and which would clearly indicate some progress in the relationship. We closed the session with John writing down a whole list of action items that he was willing to experiment with.

Solutions

When we met by accident 3 months later, John mentioned that although the situation at work was absolutely crazy, collaboration with his boss was really good. I have no information about what really helped, whether it was John's extended behavioral repertoire, his newly gained self-confidence in his capabilities to influence, or his refined perception for discovering reassuring hints from his boss's behavior. From a systemic standpoint, I would assume that every change John makes influences his interaction with other people and their reactions. From a constructivist view it might also be that John simply perceives different parts of reality and now gives increasing attention to positive signs from his boss that he overlooked before. One thing we can be sure of: John will continue to maintain his target-oriented behavior sustainably, as long as he discerns reinforcing signals from his boss.

Case Example 3: Career Decision

Sometimes the basis for decision making is very complex. The decision seems irresolvable; none of the options are really attractive enough. Director Ernest, with his most impressive banking career, sat in front of me and took almost 30 minutes to elaborate on the delicate details of his upcoming decision between two possible internal positions. He had to decide within the next 4 days. The multinational bank he worked for was in some chaos due to a reorganization. At the time, they were between the old and new organizational diagrams and there were a great many unpredictable variables.

"How can I best support you in the remaining 30 minutes of our session?" was my question.

"I don't know," he said. "With the remaining 4 days until the decision, I won't have time to work out what I'd really like for myself, anyway. You know, until now all my career moves have been driven by external circumstances. Actually, what I have really hoped for is to start taking time for myself, choose from what I want in life, shape my own life according to my own visions, but instead again I am stuck with only two options." I asked him if we should stick with this topic. He said yes, that shaping his own life was really important. I said, "Let's turn this topic into a scale between 1 and 10. Where are you now on this scale, if 10 means that you shape your life on your own?" After careful consideration he indicated 2.5, and subsequently we discussed for nearly 20 minutes the small differences between his 2.5 compared to a 1 on the scale. I repeatedly asked, "What else is already in your 2.5?" We talked about his small breakthroughs, whether at the bank or in his family, his regular athletic engagement as soccer coach for youth, and some personal successes in his relationship with his wife. I asked him which of all these things he was most proud of. He replied, "The fact that I came to see you today! I moved heaven and earth to get this appointment with you, postponed two internal meetings, drove here from Zurich, and now I am actually sitting here and I have started taking time for myself, even though it's going to cost me the whole weekend to catch up with work that I missed." I wanted to know if he needed anything else from me regarding his decision before we concluded. "No, forget about the decision. There is no such thing as a perfectly foreseeable decision anyway. Whatever I decide in the end, the main thing is for me to realize that I have actually started doing what is really important to me." With these words, he headed back to Zurich with the self-confidence of a man who had taken time for himself.

When a dilemma appears unresolvable, as coaches we can sometimes be helpful in providing another perspective and a third choice. From a mutual acquaintance, I have heard that Ernest is well along in shaping his own life.

There is no connection whatever
between the problem and the solution.
—Steve de Shazer

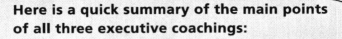

Here is a quick summary of the main points of all three executive coachings:

- Speak of capabilities instead of deficits.
- Ask about what works instead of what is missing.
- Develop ideas about the preferred future instead of analyzing the causes of the problem.
- Find out what the world looks like beyond the obstacles—starting with the end in mind.
- Use scaling questions to explore differences and tangible precursors of the solution.

The coach's contribution to the conversation is plain and simple:

1. Be persistent in searching for existing resources.
2. Tap clients on the shoulder if their view is fixed on unsolvable problems and deficits, and invite them to expand their field of vision in a more useful direction.

The particular challenge of a brief coach consists of remaining consistently simple, even when things become complex, and presupposing customer competencies even when they do not seem obvious.

We admit that keeping coaching this simple is not always easy to do. Yet the results can be highly satisfying for both coach and client.

Rolling the Dice

This is a pretending experiment for coaches who are curious about the hidden resources of their clients.

Before the next coaching session, take two dice and roll them. The first die indicates how many minutes after the session to start your experiment. The two dice together indicate how many minutes to keep doing the experiment. During the time of the experiment, act as if you really and fully believe:

- That your client brought all the necessary resources to the session
- That there is nothing that needs to be added or changed
- That your only task is to detect and reinforce existing resources and solutions

After the session, take a few minutes to reflect how things were different during the time of your experiment.

12

Beyond Technique:
Continuous Learning as a Coach

When we meet pioneers of coaching at coaching conferences, we are always impressed by the devotion and curiosity with which they continue to learn. They tell us enthusiastically about things that they are currently trying out or new discoveries in their own work. They sit in the lobby and have long conversations with participants searching for their discoveries. Their motto seems to be "you can't keep an old dog from learning new tricks." The only difference between a seasoned coach and beginner might be that depending on your experience you are currently learning different things. The more experienced you are, the less you are dealing with the techniques and procedures of coaching and the more it is about questions that transcend the solid mastery of the craft.

At the end of this book, we would like to shed some light on some of these learning fields beyond technique and give you some hints on how to broaden your own learning horizon. Some of these aspects have been defined as core competencies for professional coaches by the International Coach Federation.

Coaching presence:
The ability to be fully conscious
and create a spontaneous relationship
with the client, employing a style that
is open, flexible, and confident. The coach is present and
flexible during the coaching process, dancing in the moment,
accessing intuition, and trusting inner knowing, goes with the
gut, is open to not knowing, and takes risks.
(ICF Core Competencies)

The Art of Coaching Presence

We consider coaching presence to be the ability of the coach to improvise flexibly with what arises in the moment. Often this requires letting go of our own expectations or concepts, for example the structure of a conversation or standard questions. You can see coaching presence when the questions of the coach arise out of the answers of the customer and not vice versa, or if coach and client are exploring new territory together in their conversation. The coach does not know where the path will lead or whether it is going to be useful or not. The coach dances in the moment and is confident that this is useful. Coaches can change their own perspective and can experiment with options for their own actions.

The Art of Cocreating With the Client

The above-mentioned example also shows a second learning field beyond coaching technique: the ability of the coach to see the client not only as an expert for his or her own goal and customized solution but also as a coexpert for the further development of the coaching process.

You can see this, for example, when the coach goes with the client's flow. He might invite the client's opinion on how to continue the conversation or ask for permission to elaborate on a certain topic. If the coach is stuck, he or she can ask the client for the useful next question to ask.

A coach who masters the art of cocreation builds on the ideas and thoughts of the client to generate a truly unique coaching process.

We remember a scene from one of our workshops for advanced coaches. Lori had coached Alan, another participant. Lori started by asking Alan two questions at the beginning and then took a short pause, saying, "Oh, this is probably really not easy for you—and I can't even think of a smart question. At the moment, I can't think of how I could be useful to you." She looked at the other participant and seemed little bit helpless. Then she looked back at Alan and continued: "Can I say something? Would you be willing to change places with me?" Alan nodded, and coach and client changed places. Then Lori said, "Alan, if you were in my position as coach, which question would you ask of yourself as customer?" Alan reflected for a moment and then came up with a question. Lori answered, "Okay, how would you answer this question?" They continued with switched roles for about three more questions when Alan happily and with a sparkle in his eyes said, "We can switch places again. The coaching is finished. I have reached my goal!"

Cocreating includes keeping an eye on the overall process and thus creating and holding a safe space. "We have 10 minutes left until the end of the conversation. What would be the most useful thing that we could do in these 10 minutes?"

The Art of Letting Go

Coaches sometimes have the idea that they have to ask exquisitely ingenious questions or influence a large change in the customer to be worth their money. This idea somehow attaches to our minds and creates exactly the opposite. Letting this idea go is a real art form. One of the ICF's coaching competencies is defined as follows: acting free of any expectations toward oneself, the customer, and the coaching.

You only have your hands free
if you don't keep a firm
grip on everything.

Letting go can be seen in the moments when the coach doesn't do anything but be there with the customer, when it is possible to let the client be without having to contribute one's own important and smart thoughts as a coach. Sometimes just being a witness for the client's learning and progress is all it really takes.

Letting go also helps us work with the necessary humility. Humility teaches us that the only thing we can do is confidently and elegantly create a framework in which customers can find their own learning, their first steps, their solution—nothing more.

Coaching in Action:
Beyond Technique

To illustrate how coaching can be conducted beyond technique, we would like to show you some excerpts from a conversation that our colleague Jürgen Hargens had with a coaching client named Klaus. The coaching happened in 2005 at one of our live coaching days in Switzerland as a demonstration for our practitioners.

When you read the dialogue you will recognize many of the above-mentioned learning fields—and maybe even a few additional ones.

Excerpt from the beginning of the coaching:

Jürgen: Good. So if this is successful, this coaching, as we call it, do you then know where you want to go? Do you know whether this is a good step for you? So what needs to happen in the end so that you can say "good"?

Klaus: No, I don't know where it should go. No.

Jürgen: Okay. So if you take a step—it might be that you will be shoved a little bit today—so if you move just a little bit, how will you notice that this was exactly the right thing to do?

Klaus: I would be calmer.

Jürgen: Calmer . . .

Klaus: Yes.

Jürgen: Okay. How else are you going to notice?

Klaus: No, it's really a question of my emotional state.

Jürgen: Okay. And what does your emotional state look like when you've taken this step?

Klaus: It has something to do with being calm and relaxed.

Jürgen: Okay, so what are the effects of noticing or feeling this calm and relaxation? How will your wife notice—wow, Klaus has taken a step.

Klaus: Yes, you would notice that.

Jürgen: And how is your wife going to notice?

Klaus: She will think: He might have a different way of tackling things and that's what I notice. And then there are all these small steps in different directions. And a big step is the calm that I'm feeling then.

Jürgen: Ah, yes. Good, I can see that. Start moving, gain some experience, and then calm down.

Klaus: Yes.

Jürgen: Good. So how could it be useful for you somehow today?

Klaus: I can't think of anything, actually. No, I don't really know at the moment.

Jürgen: Yeah, I know. This question . . . well, it sounds so simple and then you
start thinking: If I only knew. Difficult to know.
Klaus: Yeah.

Appreciative reflection for this clarification of the contract by Jürgen:

- We were impressed by how closely Jürgen's questions follow the
customer and how consistently and easily he manages to do that. He
builds a question directly on Klaus's answers and uses the expression
and metaphors Klaus uses, all the while remaining persistent and
caring.
- Jürgen shows a lot of appreciation and understanding for Klaus's
thinking process and ideas. And when Klaus cannot answer a question, Jürgen manages to make this look very normal—which, in
effect, it is. This is how he manages to keep up the conversation and
the trusting relationship.
- Jürgen takes time to carefully negotiate a contract. He only moves
on to the next step in the conversation when it is clear to Klaus and
also to him how the coaching could be useful for him. This is a
wonderful example of the art of not knowing.

Excerpt from the middle of the conversation:

Klaus: So this is one of these concrete steps . . .
Jürgen: Yes.
Klaus: That would be possible.
Jürgen: Well, not only one that would be possible. Maybe it isn't even really
possible, but one that you really feel like taking.
Klaus: Ah yes, exactly.
Jürgen: More like this: Oh wow, whether you take it or not, whether it's realistic or not doesn't matter. It's one that you feel like taking.
Klaus: This is so difficult.

Jürgen: Yup—feeling like doing something is sometimes really difficult.

Klaus: Extremely difficult.

Jürgen: Yes.

Klaus: I have an idea . . .

Jürgen: Okay . . .

Klaus: It has something to do with time. I feel like having more time for everything. Is that something, or is that not a step?

Jürgen: Why not?

Klaus: Time is something external. I will take a step—just give me time. Full stop.

Jürgen: Okay, time. How much would you like?

Klaus: Enough.

Jürgen: How much is enough? So tomorrow. Tomorrow's Tuesday. How much time would you like to have on top of the 24 hours that you have tomorrow?

Klaus: Yeah, right, that's great!

Jürgen: Maybe you would like to take some away so that you only have 20 hours. Could that be?

Klaus: That could also be. Yes, that's the difficulty . . .

Jürgen: Sure. If everything was so simple, you probably would have done it already.

Klaus: Then I would have already solved it, yes.

Jürgen: Exactly. And now we're sitting here . . .

Klaus: And when I now say that I need 5 hours more, or 10 hours more or 24 hours more, then, I think I would probably like more.

Jürgen: Probably more, okay. How much more would you feel like having?

Klaus: Five hours.

Jürgen: Five hours, okay. Let me have a look . . . oh yeah, here I still have 5 hours left.

(Jürgen rummages through his pockets and takes out one hand as if he was holding something and carefully hands it over to Klaus, who takes it.)

Klaus: Super . . .

Jürgen: Can you see? Let me hand them to you . . .

Klaus: How nice of you!

Jürgen: They are for tomorrow.

Klaus: Thanks.

Jürgen: Good. Now I'm curious. What are you going to do with these 5 hours?"

Klaus: Okay, tomorrow it's like this. I get up and then I look to see whether my son is already up.

Jürgen: Okay. How old is he?

Klaus: He is three and a half.

Jürgen: Oh, really, and he sleeps through the night?

Klaus: Yeah, he sleeps well. Sometimes he sleeps too long and I think, wake up. But I don't wake him up. Then I would simply give him half an hour of my 5. I would then have 4.5 hours left and that would be enough. So I think he could sleep for another half hour, like today, and then I am . . .

Jürgen: If your son sleeps another half hour that you give him, what you do with this half hour? Do you stand at his bedside and admire him, or what do you do?

Klaus: Exactly, that's a good question. Actually this is the first hour that is given to me and him because I start the morning calm and not like: go go go!

Jürgen: Yes.

Klaus: I already experienced this today.

Jürgen: Really?

Klaus: Yeah, I should have . . . but today was like tomorrow, because . . .

Jürgen: Well, then I can take back that hour, if you want . . .

Klaus: He slept an hour longer than usual and I let him and read the newspaper.

Jürgen: Ah.

Klaus: And that was great. It was great, but I wasn't feeling really well because I knew that I should have . . . well, actually, around a quarter to seven I woke him up and then we went to nursery school at quarter past 8. And today he slept in until 10 minutes to 8. And I let him. For me, everything was calm. I was sitting in the garden, drinking coffee, reading the newspaper. . . . Of course there were a lot of things that I could have done . . .

Jürgen: But you did do a lot of things: you read a newspaper, had some coffee, sat in the garden . . .

Our appreciation:

- It is impressive how Jürgen deals with the spontaneous idea of "5 hours" that he found in his pocket by accident. He creates a preferred future that really fits the situation. There is so much sense of humor and playfulness, which enables the customer to develop new perspectives.
- Jürgen invites his customer to increase his choices with a wonderful ease and playfulness. He positions his invitations in such a way that the customer can easily say no and let them go if they do not fit.
- Jürgen completely trusts the customer as expert not only for the solution but also for the end of the conversation. The customer decides when it is good enough and Jürgen can agree appreciatively (see below).

Exerpt from the end of the conversation:

Jürgen: Your son probably also sleeps in because he thinks about all the mischief he will be doing today.
Klaus: True.
Jürgen: Good. We only have a limited time for this coaching, yet we are still somehow in the middle of it.
Klaus: Yes.
Jürgen: My question is now: What would you like to talk about? What do you still need or can we finish at this point?
Klaus: Ooff!
Jürgen: Another difficult question!
Klaus: Yes, this is a difficult question. But I think we can let it stand as it is. I think I'm rather finished here.

Jürgen: I have an idea how you can probably find out.

Klaus: Please, yes.

Jürgen: You are talking about steps and becoming calmer. I would like to ask you to get up and walk back and forth. Sit down again and then I'll ask you again.

Klaus: Good.

Jürgen: Okay, Klaus. Is this now a point where we can let things rest, or are you still missing something, or do you still need something else?

Klaus: Mmm, what should I do . . .

Jürgen: Still difficult, hmm?

Klaus: Yes, we can leave it at that.

Jürgen: Okay, so we will leave it at that. Thank you very much.

Klaus: This is good work.

Jürgen: And, Klaus, please take good care of the four hours that you still have from me.

Klaus: Of course, thanks.

Jürgen: Thank you very much. Thank you.

And with this example of the close of the coaching conversation, we will leave you. Thank you for reading this far. With a last experiment (below), we wish you good luck. Goodbye.

Multiscaling Competencies

Our colleague Evan George from BRIEF Consultancy in London developed a simple tool for regular reflection on your learning and for determining where you stand with regard to your competencies.

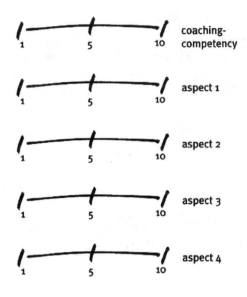

Five competency scales.

Establish the Scales

- On a scale from 1 to 10, where do you stand in your general coaching competency?
- Name subscales for four relevant parts of your general competency, for example, in respect to your ability to be brief and effective. Where do you stand on each of those four subscales?

Appreciate the Distance Already Traveled

- On the general scale, how is your competency different now than it was at 1? How did you manage to move from 1 to where you are now?
- On each of the subscales, what do you do differently now compared to at 1? What else? Remember a recent moment of excellence. Where do you put that on the scale? How did you act differently then?

Defining Clues of Upcoming Progress

- Go through each of the scales again and define one or two things that will make you notice that you have moved 1 point up on the scale. How will your clients notice that you have moved 1 point up?

The Authors Answer
a Small Potpourri of
Frequently Asked Questions

Daniel Meier, Peter Szabó, and translator Kirsten Dierolf answer some frequently asked questions from customers, clients, coaching colleagues, friends, acquaintances, and relatives.

Authors Daniel Meier and Peter Szabó.

How did you come up with the name Solutionsurfers?

K. D.: I guess Peter must have had the sound of the word *Ghostbusters* from the 80s movie in his ears. Solutionsurfers has the same rhythm to it.

P. S.: I really liked that movie! But until now I always thought the name Solutionsurfers came from my passion for surfing waves on a surfboard. I am fascinated with how an entire new generation is moving through life on their snowboards, skateboards, and surfboards. It is a more playful and adaptable way of dealing with ups and downs and making the best use of the terrain.

D. M.: Also I think the name Solutionsurfers beautifully expresses the idea of surfing on existing solutions by making use of the natural forward-moving power that is already in place.

Who are your role models?

P. S.: There are a few special people that I admire a lot: the coaching pioneers Timothy Gallway and Sir John Whitmore, and naturally Steve de Shazer and Insoo Kim Berg, to whom I owe the solution-focused change paradigm. I am very grateful that I was able to meet all of them personally. With them, I had fascinating aha moments, when I thought, can it really be this simple? And if it can, this is what I want to learn and explore!

D. M.: Apart from these pioneers, the participants in our workshops are always role models for me. Especially when I see how much curiosity and flexibility they have as well as a mix of ease and seriousness as they learn and coach.

K. D.: My role models are Insoo and Steve and all the brilliant master coaches that I have been able to observe (including some present here). For me it's not about following a technique but about being solution focused in the broadest sense: concentrating on the clients' goals, staying clear of interpretations and assumptions, dancing in the moment, and trusting in the interaction.

Are some professions more suitable than others for those who want to become coaches? Psychologist, teacher, salesperson?

D. M.: I once was preparing the workshop room together with a good colleague and was looking for some Scotch tape [winks to P. S.]. He was rummaging through his pockets and then said with some hilarity: "The most important thing in life is love—and the second most important is Scotch tape." and that's also what I think about the prerequisites of becoming a coach. There are probably no ideal conditions for becoming a coach. What is most important for me is that you feel and live appreciation, respect, or love for people (for yourself and others). My personal path to coaching was via pedagogy, adult education, music, and some years of leadership experience.

P. S.: Having leadership experience is something that we have in common. It really helps us when we coach in the business world. I started out as a lawyer and then worked many years in human resource management before I founded my own company as a coach and trainer of coaches.

K. D. [smiles]: Of course, as any management consultant, trainer, and coach knows, there is only one way to become a good coach. You need to be a linguist and recovering theologian! No—actually, what I think is very useful is if you are willing to learn the grammar of an organization, a field, an industry, a culture, a client, so that you can converse on the client's turf without loosing your grip on your own ground. Insoo always said, "One step in the client's world and one step in your own." For me it's important to have my own world so that I can add to the client's by useful differentiation.

How can you build your career as a coach?

K. D.: I've been running Marketing for Coaches workshops for a while—and for me the most important thing seems to be that if you want to be come a coach, you should coach. Don't spend time on flyers, home pages, business cards, and all the other things that you think you need. Get your first 50 to 100 coaching sessions in (paid or unpaid), find the natural habitat of your preferred clients, tell them stories about how you made a difference as a coach and about the other wonderful people you had the honor to coach (without naming them, of course), and I am sure you will have a good chance to develop a practice.

Do you think certification or graduating from a coaching school plays a big role?

P. S.: I believe that continuous learning as a coach is a key to success. Proper training and going through a certification process are good opportunities to understand where you are in your learning. Also more and more corporate clients expect professional certification, for example, by the International Coach Federation or a similar organization. Nevertheless, the added value for your clients is in the quality of the coaching you do, and not in the certificates hanging on your wall.

What does brief coaching look like at home, at the kitchen table? Are there daily examples for solution-focused, successful conversations—say, with kids at puberty or with mothers-in-law?

D. M.: This is an interesting question. I think I am very careful with coaching at home even though sometimes I can't help myself, and a coaching question slips out. It might sound like this:

Son (12 years old): Oh, I'm fed up with doing my homework. All these calculations!

Dad-Coach: What would you rather do instead of doing your homework?

Son (15 years old): You and your coaching questions. Coach someone who pays you for it!

Dad-Coach: Oh, sorry. I didn't want to ask a coaching question.

Son (12 years old): I don't want anything different, but I want you to see that doing homework is really hard work. You can simply sit there and read.

Son (15 years old): On a scale of 1 to 10, how strenuous is that at the moment?

Dad-Coach: Now you are coaching!

Son (15 years old): I just wanted to show you that I can do it!

Son (12 years old): Today it's really at an 8.

Dad-Coach: "Wow, that's really high. But still, how come it's only an 8 and not a 10? That would be worse.

Son (12 years old): Okay, we did talk about the homework at school. I know how to do it. Now I just have to finish it and the longer we are talking here, the longer it takes. So please shut up!

P. S.: I also had a very touching and nice example with my 13-year-old daughter that I wrote down. You can download it at www.solution-surfers.com under Resources by the title, "Dad Can You Coach Me?" And I share Daniel's reluctance. At home I prefer to be husband or father or friend and not coach.

K. D.: I agree. My kids also cringe when I try to coach them. I remember a wonderful example, though, that really touched me and that has changed something in how I am dealing with my kids, what I focus on. I once visited my coaching trainer before a course [smiles at Peter] and the youngest of the family was just coming home from a friend's house on a dreary autumn day. He was crying: "Dad, it's so dark outside. I was so scared." My impulse would have been to do a motherly "poor rabbit" move. The loving father put his arm around his boy and said, "And you managed to come back home in the dark even though you were so scared. How bold and brave of you! How did you do that?" The son stopped crying immediately and started telling the story about how he ran from streetlamp to streetlamp.

Does the effect of brief coaching depend on culture? Does this model also work in China?

P. S.: The book that Insoo and I have written has actually been translated into Mandarin. So far I have not noticed any dependency on culture. A respectful, appreciative, and affirmative attitude seems to be helpful in all the places I have worked at so far.

What also helps is that the model is extremely client centered. I notice that when I'm outside of Switzerland, I take special care to ask what fits for my customers and participants. Generally, I think that intercultural adaptation simply needs the same care as the adaptation between two different people of the same culture.

Speaking of traveling, are there weekends this year when you are at home?

D. M.: If I work on weekends, I take Monday and Tuesday off. But it really doesn't happen very often. What cannot be prevented, however, is staying in hotels during the week—and there are quite a few nights that I'm not at home. On the other hand, Peter and I take enough vacation time during the year and spend it with our families.

K. D.: I'm home most weekends, except when I am training solution-focused consultants. However, I am far behind Daniel and Peter in learning how to not work. I'll manage one day, I'm sure, maybe, I guess, probably, sometime . . .

P. S.: I also do a lot of international traveling on weekends. However, I am proud to say that lately the weekends that I am at home have really been free of work. That definitely wasn't the case in the first 10 years of starting this business. I am somewhat surprised by my freshly gained, confident peace of mind. It's almost like a miracle.

Do you really believe in miracles?

D. M. and K. D.: Sure!

P. S.: In miracles that happen with and without coaching.

And what else do you believe in?

D. M.: That the solution-focused approach will continue to spread slowly and will contribute to more ease in the business world. That words create reality.

K. D.: In my clients.

P. S.: That our desires are the precursors of our capabilities.

Bibliography
and Helpful Web Sites

Books on Solution-Focused Coaching

Berg, Insoo Kim and Peter Szabo. *Brief Coaching for Lasting Solutions.* W. W. Norton and Company, 2005.

Berg, Insoo Kim, and Peter De Jong. *Interviewing for Solutions.* Cengage Learning Services, 2007.

Cauffman, Louis, and Kirsten Dierolf. *The Solution Tango: Seven Simple Steps to Solutions in Management.* Cyan Books, 2006.

Jackson, Paul Z., and Mark McKergow. *The Solutions Focus: Making Coaching and Change SIMPLE.* Nicholas Brealey, 2006.

McKergow, Mark, and Jenny Clarke, eds. *Solutions Focus Working.* SolutionsBooks, 2006.

Meier, Daniel. *Team Coaching With the Solution Circle: A Practical Guide to Solutions Focused Team Development.* SolutionsBooks, 2005.

Röhrig, Peter, ed. *Solution Tools.* SolutionsBooks, 2008.

Other Books on Coaching

Gallway, W. Timothy. *The Inner Game of Work: Focus, Learning, Pleasure and Mobility in the Workplace.* Random House, 2001.

Orem, Sara L., Jacqueline Binkert, and Ann L. Clancy. *Appreciative Coaching: A Positive Process for Change.* Jossey-Bass, 2007.

Whitmore, John. *Coaching for Performance: Growing People, Performance and Purpose.* Nicholas Brealey, 2002.

Links
Coaching in General

International Coach Federation. Web site with links to coaches all over the world, information about ICF certification and international conferences. www.coachfederation.org

European Mentoring and Coaching Council. Web site with conferences, journal, and quality award. www.emccouncil.org

Solution-Focused Work

International Association of Solution Focused Coaches, Consultants and Trainers. Web site with the most complete resources about solution-focused work in organizations. www.asfct.org

SolutionCircle. Solution focused work with teams. www.solutioncircle.com

Solutionsurfers. Peter Szabó and Daniel Meier offer internationally accredited coach trainings in Switzerland and hold workshops worldwide. www.solutionsurfers.com

SolutionsAcademy. Information on solution focus and solution-focused consulting services. www.solutionsacademy.com

sfwork. New solution-focused books in English. www.sfwork.com

*solution*surfers®

Brief Coach Training

9 day residential course in Basel, Switzerland with Peter Szabó and an international faculty. Training program accredited by the ICF.

www.solutionsurfers.com